COLLEGE TRIPWIRES
READY OR NOT
Stories from the Students Behind the Statistics

PRICHARD COMMITTEE FOR ACADEMIC EXCELLENCE

With a Foreword from
Dr. Vicki Phillips

© 2017 Prichard Committee for Academic Excellence

All rights reserved. This book or any portion thereof may not be reproduced or used in any manner whatsoever without the express written permission of the Prichard Committee except in brief quotations or other fair use under US copyright law.

The names of students and others in this book have been changed to protect their privacy, except for Student Voice Team members Rainesford Stauffford and Kevin Short, the Grissom Scholars, and Neomia Hagans, with their consent or, for minors, their parent's consent. The views expressed in this publication not written by the Student Voice Team or its Editors are those of the original author and do not necessarily represent those of the Prichard Committee or the Student Voice Team.

Second Printing October 2017
Paperback

ISBN 978-0-9677756-0-9 (Paperback)
ISBN 978-0-9677756-1-6 (Ebook)
ISBN 978-0-9677756-2-3 (Facilitator Edition)

Published by the Prichard Committee for Academic Excellence
271 W. Short St., Suite 202
Lexington, KY 40507

Printed in the USA

Contact the Student Voice Team about discounts for bulk orders at studentvoiceteam@prichardcommittee.org

Book & cover design by Hiatt Allen

Front & back cover photo by Andrew Krech, Associated Press, used with permission.
All other back cover photos by the Student Voice Team.

The text of this book is set in Crimson Roman, a font by Sebastian Kosch. The headings of this book are set in Muli Light, a font by Vernon Adams. The title of this book is set in Montserrat Medium, a font by Julieta Ulanovsky. All fonts have an Open Font License.

State Farm Youth Advisory Board and Lumina Foundation logos used with permission. The views expressed in this publication are those of the Student Voice Team or the original author and do not necessarily represent those of the State Farm Youth Advisory Board, including its officers or employees, or the Lumina Foundation, including its officers or employees.

Publisher's Cataloging-in-Publication data

Names: Student Voice Team, author. | Phillips, Vicki, foreword author.

Title: Ready or not: stories from the students behind the statistics / Student Voice Team; foreword by Phillips, Vicki.

Description: Includes bibliographical references. | Lexington, KY: Prichard Committee for Academic Excellence, 2017.

Identifiers: ISBN 978-0-9677756-0-9 | LCCN 2017947371

Subjects: LCSH College preparation programs—United States—Kentucky—Case studies. | Academic achievement—United States—Kentucky. | College attendance—United States—Kentucky. | Education—Aims and objectives—United States. | Educational equalization. | Education, Higher—United States. | Universities and colleges. | BISAC EDUCATION/ Educational Policy & Reform/General | EDUCATION/Higher

Classification: LCC LC213.2.S78 2017 | DDC 378.1/61—dc23

To our fellow students
& those who always believed
our voices matter.

This book and College Tripwires project was underwritten with generous grants from the State Farm Youth Advisory Board & the Lumina Foundation and its Strategy Labs.

Contents

Contributors	vii
About Us	viii
Foreword	xiii
Preface	xix
The Misnavigateds	1
Zach	5
Emma	11
Tabitha	19
Tyler	25
The Givens	33
Ajay	37
Blair	43
Matt	49
Alice	55
Robert	61
Rainesford	67
The Dismissers	75
Charlie	79
Connor	85
Joseph	91
Lilian	97
Claire	103
The Moonlighters	109
Brianna, Cate, Dalia, Kadisha, Madison & Natasha	113
Mackenzie	127
Brianna	133
Suzie	141
The Newcomers	149
Dhonu, David, Maaria & Sal	153
Zainab & Imani	167
The Oddsbuckers	179
Jordan	183
Akhil	189
Elizabeth	199
Jule	207
Hiba	213
Heather	221

Kevin	227	*Dylan*	281
Danielle	233	*The Parents, the Counselor*	
Grissom Scholars	241	*& the Principal*	287
The Village	249	Afterword	299
Neomia	253	Acknowledgments	305
Ms. Paceley	263	Glossary	311
Ms. Henly	269	Notes	317
Paul	277		

Contributors

Executive Editors

Sahar Mohammadzadeh
Student Director, Postsecondary Research & Outreach

Rachel Burg Belin
*Student Voice Team Director,
Prichard Committee for Academic Excellence*

Publishing Editor

Hiatt Allen

Associate Editors

Perry Allen	Eliza Jane Schaeffer
Meredith Crockett	Jamie Smith
Gentry Fitch	Laney Taylor
Maddy Jenkins	Amanda Wahlstedt

College Tripwires Team

Sneha Amrit	Mollie Pope
Sarah Belin	Emanuelle Sippy
Amanda Byerman	Zachariah Sippy
Iishe Davis	Emma Stivers
Lily Gardner	Allison Tu
Leighanne Guettler-James	Henry Walther
Rosalyn Huff	Colton Williams
Nasim Mohammadzadeh	Stephanie Yang
Pearl Morttey	Logan Zeigler

About Us

The Student Voice Team is a student-led initiative of the Prichard Committee for Academic Excellence. Consisting of over one hundred self-selected youth from across Kentucky, we work to integrate students as research, policy, and advocacy partners in the efforts to improve our schools.

In 2014, we helped restore public school funding in Kentucky to pre-recession levels. During the 2015 legislative session, we advocated for the inclusion of students on superintendent screening committees. Later that year, we released *Uncovering the Tripwires to Postsecondary Success*, an examination of college transitions, and completed our first Student Voice Audit, modeling ways students and other stakeholders can improve their school's learning climate.

In 2016, we led the Powerball Promise campaign, successfully advocating for the restoration of scholarships for over eight thousand students from low-income families. That summer, we released *Students As Partners: Integrating Student Voice in the Governing Bodies of Kentucky Schools*, a report providing recommendations for how schools can include students in their decision-making process. That fall, and during the following school year, we took *Students As Partners* on the road and put it into action, convening students, teachers, and administrators in schools across the state to discuss the value of student voice integration.

Also throughout the entire 2016-17 school year, we continued our College Tripwires research, talking to students for the purpose of this book and surveying them for *Ready or Not: The Statistics Behind the Stories*, an original data report. In the coming months, we will continue our efforts to amplify and elevate the voices of students to inform education decisions, with a special emphasis on young people who are least heard in our school system.

The Student Voice Team
2012–2017

Brooke Abell	Tsage Douglas	Sara Khandani	Rhadika Sharma
John David Adams	Nathan Eapen	Young Kyung Kim	Milo Sheinfeld
Faizan Ahmed	Marie Emedi	Meghana Kudrimoti	Eumin Shin
Monica Alden	Quin Endicott	Lucy Kurtz	Kevin Short
Rosemary Alden	Jijie Fan	Christian Lauritzen	Emanuelle Sippy
Hiatt Allen	Devynn Fergerson	Fabian Leon	Zachariah Sippy
Perry Allen	Nicole Fielder	Eleanor Liu	Jamie Smith
Sneha Amrit	Gentry Fitch	Jasmine Liu	Reagan Smith
Maggie Back	Eli Flomenhoft	Jeliah Logan	Susie Smith
Stephanie Bamfo	Lily Gardner	Nancy LoGuidice	Taylor Smith
Bella Beilman	Erin Glynn	Stephanie Lopez	Madeline Springate
Sarah Belin	Claire Gothard	Emma Li Matthews	Rainesford Stauffer
Linzie Ashton Bishop	Leighanne Guettler-James	Nathaniel Messer	Emily Steele
Anne Boggess	Mahika Gupta	Mikayla Mitchell	Callaway Stivers
Ross Boggess	Keith Guy	Nasim Mohammadzadeh	Emma Stivers
Sadie Bograd	Eric Hagan	Sahar Mohammadzadeh	Dustin Summers
Isaac Boss	Lauren Hall	Allie Monck	Tony Sun
Allington Bowling	Meg Hancock	Pearl Morttey	Sam Swayze
Michaela Bowman	Lauren Hart	Mariah Mowbray	Faith Tallaferro
Jack Bradley	Evan Hayes	Malcolm Murray	Izzy Taylor
Rachel Bradley	Angeline He	Sahil Nair	Laney Taylor
Sophia Brannen	Christopher Heinrich	Joi Ogbulu	Tiana Thé
Andrew Brennen	Lauren Hemenover	Santiago O'Neil	Zach Thornton
Khamari Brooks	Hope Henderson	Madison Ortega	Don Trowell
Lydia Burns	Desmond Howard	Cheyenne Osuala	Allison Tu
Amanda Byerman	Rosalyn Huff	Mollie Pope	Carmen Maria von Unrug
Will Byerman	Justin Huffman	Gabrielle Price	Chaze Vinci
Kaili Carson	Daniel Hurt	Morgan Rehm	Reilly Voit
Alora Chesney	Nicholas Imam	Parin Rekhraj	Amanda Wahlstedt
Gabriel Chesney	Michael Jarman	Silja Richter	Henry Walther
Erin Christopher	Maddy Jenkins	Dylan Ruddy	Lauren Watson
Eleanor Clifton	Zoe Jenkins	Abhi Saraff	Taylor Whitaker
Leea Collard	Seth Jessie	Eliza Jane Schaeffer	Colton Williams
Meredith Crockett	John Kellen	Jonathan Schaeffer	Cameron Wright
Cate Cunningham	Naomi Kellogg	Kayla Seamands	Stephanie Yang
Iishe Davis	Akhil Kesaraju	Amani Shalash	Logan Zeigler
Sydney Delaney	Rohith Kesaraju	Anjali Shankar	Aidan Ziliak

Rachel Burg Belin
Director

About the Prichard Committee

The Prichard Committee for Academic Excellence is an independent, non-partisan citizens' advocacy group. Comprised of volunteer civic and business leaders from across Kentucky, the Committee has worked to improve education for Kentuckians of all ages since 1983.

*"Maybe stories are just
data with a soul."*

Dr. Brené Brown

Foreword

Over the last few years, I have watched with growing pride and respect the evolution of the Prichard Committee Student Voice Team. It started with a small, eager-to-make-a-difference group of like-minded young people with similar stories and aspirations. Now it's a movement embracing the diversity of perspectives and experiences that is Kentucky.

The team knew even in their early days that the charge to have student perspectives influence the strategies for improving Kentucky's schools would require raising voices not typically heard. They committed to becoming authentic listeners and storytellers as well as tireless advocates so that tomorrow's opportunities for Kentucky's youth will be better than yesterday's.

It's a commitment that I feel personally—one that is rooted in my own Kentucky experience. I was raised in Kentucky, went to school in Kentucky, worked and taught in Kentucky, was launched from Kentucky. I have gone on to serve in a number of roles in education—superintendent, state commissioner of education, director of K-12 education at the world's largest foundation. In each role, I have had this burning desire to give back, to do my part to make sure that every child in America gets the opportunity that I almost didn't.

Like the name of the place I grew up, Falls of Rough, Kentucky, my path to college was rough. I grew up on a small farm where we raised pigs, grew vegetables, hunted for our supper and had an outhouse in our back yard. We had a strong work ethic and a commitment to community. I worked on the farm, wandered the woods, waded in the creeks, and fixed wounded birds and animals. I gained a sense of what it is like to grow up in a rural area where we fend for ourselves and try to help out our neighbors.

But there wasn't much in the way of expectations for someone from the poor end of our county, like me. No one in my family had ever gone to college. My grades put me near the top of my class, but no one talked to me about continuing my education past high school.

Then I met a peer from the upper, more affluent, end of the county who insisted that I was as smart as she was and should be thinking about college. She wasn't willing to accept that the gap between where we grew up would determine where we ended up. So she pushed me to take the ACT, which I had never heard of, and get small scholarships, which I had never heard of, and apply to college, which I had barely heard of.

When I told my family, I was going to college, my stepfather told me: "If you go to college, you are not my daughter; your values are not our values. Don't plan on coming back." I went anyway, and when I got there, I wasn't ready.

My English professor handed back my first paper, my first F, and said, "This is not what I expected."

My Statistics professor handed back a low grade on my first test and said, "I hadn't figured you for this."

You see, I made those good grades in high school on memory and rote learning. I knew how to diagram a complex sentence, but I didn't know how to write that sentence in an essay. I knew how to follow the steps shown by the teacher to solve for x, but I never learned that Algebra problems are just ways of showing that two expressions are equivalent. I was drilled in the small mechanics, but I was never taught the big concepts. I was taught how to follow directions but not how to find my way when I got lost.

I made it—but not in the normal way. I got to college because I had a high school classmate from an affluent family who thought I should have the same chances she did. I made it through college because I had professors who believed I had talent that wasn't showing up in the bad grades they gave me. Before I was any of the roles on my resume, I was a poor kid who caught a lucky break and got the opportunity to bridge the gap between what I was expected to do and what I was capable of doing.

The Prichard Committee Student Voice Team is focused on helping close that gap for all of Kentucky's youth. They have studied the research, looked at effective practice, and talked to countless educators and decision makers in the state and across the country. They know that the knowledge and skills necessary to leave high school college ready are also the skills necessary to obtain a good job and advance in a career; that increasing access to college and good jobs increases economic prosperity, creates capable citizens, and lifts everybody up. They also know that in our quest to improve education, we often fail to seek the perspective of the very people we intend to serve. Recent research has shown us that some of the most valid and reliable perspectives of what happens in our classrooms and schools is that of students. So they are working to raise the voices of Kentucky's youth, in particular those seldom heard.

Inside the pages of this book, you will meet students with challenging stories and circumstances, students for whom opportunity should not be left to luck. Early in my career, I had the privilege to be part of the team charged with the initial implementation of the Kentucky Education Reform Act of 1990. KERA set the state on a new path and Kentucky should be rightfully proud of how far it has come on that journey. But these stories illustrate with raw candor the importance of not wavering from that commitment—of not forgetting the faces behind the numbers and for continuing to relentlessly seek a high quality education for each of the state's young citizens.

Don't look back; don't falter. May the voices herein strengthen your resolve.

Dr. Vicki Phillips
President and Teacher-in-Chief, TeachingPartners

Preface

About five years ago, on a colorful fall day, a dozen members of our newly-formed Student Voice Team gathered around a table in Central Kentucky to discuss the role of education in our lives. We wanted to explore ways our parent organization, the Prichard Committee for Academic Excellence, could integrate students into their work to improve Kentucky schools.

Back then, all of us were in a similar place. All of us expected to go to college. And as high school upperclassmen writing admissions essays, prepping for the ACT, and generally stressing about where we would go next after graduation, we were immersed in preparations to do just that.

To us, it was a given that college was critical. We wanted to meet basic family and community expectations. And we knew from our research that compared to people with just a high school degree, those with a college education tend to be wealthier and healthier, have more job opportunities, are more likely to do volunteer work, and have larger and more diverse business and social networks. These advantages also make people significantly better positioned to break the cycle of generational poverty.

So the idea of "college readiness," a concept bandied about by our teachers and administrators, was more than a catchphrase; it resonated with us.

But it also made us wonder about some other research we found. Why, for example, were so many students either not making it to college or dropping out once they got there? And more to the point: If so many people in our own world were on board with the importance of preparing for college, what was getting in the way of so many other Kentucky students?

That's when we decided we would hit the road to talk with more of our peers about their experiences preparing for life after high school.

One of our first field trips was to an after-school program that targeted young people from low-income backgrounds. It was there that we met Robbie, whose story became one we still can't shake.

With little prompting, Robbie told us that on most days, he didn't know where his next meal would come from. He went on to explain that if he were able to sell enough empty soda bottles to recycling centers, he would be able to buy some extra food to make sure he and his siblings ate that night.

Unlike most of his family, Robbie eventually managed to graduate from high school. But he told us that though he loved learning, he knew he would never go to college. He couldn't bear the thought of leaving his mother alone to care for his younger brothers and sisters.

We asked ourselves then: What is college readiness to students like Robbie? How can we expect students like him, who are burdened by meeting basic needs, to begin to focus on the things that consumed us, like college admissions tests and applications?

When we took those questions to a few teachers we knew, our friends from Teach for America Appalachia suggested we visit more schools to gain context and perspective. As new teachers themselves and as young people just a few years older than we were, they felt doing that was so essential, they even helped to arrange our next trip.

In Knox Central High School, we listened as some of our counterparts explained that they felt trapped in a culture of stagnation, expected to stay at home and work where their parents—and often generations before them—had lived their whole lives. We listened, too, as other students there told us that they didn't feel trapped at all but instead embraced a county and culture they never wanted to leave.

We were struck not only by the differences between our own perspectives and the students we interviewed, but also by the differences among students in Knox Central themselves. The experience reminded us that despite the way we sometimes think about our education system, the people it serves are not a monolithic mass.

Hearing these unvarnished stories sparked what became our signature strategy in an investigation ultimately involving thousands more students and spanning many of our own high-school-to-college transitions.

We made a commitment then to listen to more students, more often, from more communities across Kentucky. We would amplify and elevate student voices well beyond our own, doing whatever we could to provide platforms to ensure that decision-makers could listen and respond to them.

Above all, we were determined to hear directly from Kentucky's least-heard students. We wanted to learn more about their experiences as young people transitioning from the K-12 system. We wanted to know what they thoughtpolicymakers could learn from their stories. We wanted to listen to the primary stakeholders—those who had spent the past twelve years, the majority of their lives, living and breathing our schools—about what was and was not working as they prepared to make the leap after graduation.

These early conversations and the subsequent research they inspired and informed became the core of our first report, *Uncovering the Tripwires to Postsecondary Success*. In it, we married research with real-time student voice, highlighting the obstacles and inequities inherent in Kentucky's postsecondary transition process.

Since those early interviews, we have grown our team, developing a significantly more diverse membership: over one hundred students in elementary school through college from over thirty Kentucky counties, along with a burgeoning network of adult allies. We have also collected more student voices and shared them in local and national presentations with educators, advocates, business leaders, and policymakers. And we received added encouragement that we were on to something in 2016, when the "Powerball Promise" campaign we facilitated, fueled by the stories we collected from students struggling to afford college and involving a coalition of organizations, led to the restoration of millions of dollars of state lottery funds to need-based college scholarships.

Much has happened in the five years since those initial conversations around a table in Lexington, yet we continue to explore what students think about the way the system supports them to succeed within and beyond high school.

And that is what has brought us to this book.

It was August of 2015 when we first connected with GEAR UP Kentucky, a federal grant program coordinated by the Council for Postsecondary Education that aims to build a sustainable, college-going culture in schools with a high percentage of students from low-income households. Through that partnership, we were able to target five Kentucky high schools in five different regions representing the geographic diversity of the state for the bulk of the Student Voice Team-facilitated roundtables and interviews that appear in these pages. Also included, though, are roundtables and interviews with high school seniors and recent graduates from another eight counties spread throughout the state outside of GEAR UP's purview, plus a few students who have recently graduated high school and a few key adults who are well past their college years. All students and adults we interviewed understood their story would be used publicly, but with identifying information removed and names changed. However, a few students and adults agreed to leaving their name and identifying information when it was necessary to help readers better understand the context of their powerful stories.

At each school, we began by telling the students to separate themselves into roundtable groups of five to seven people, encouraging them to stay with friends if they wanted. We told them that as peers, we would be leading the discussion and that though we would be asking a lot of questions and recording them with our phones, there could be no wrong answers. Their comfort level was our top priority.

We kept a special eye out for two types of students in particular to pull aside into a smaller interview room: the quiet ones who had yet to say a word in the first thirty minutes or so of the roundtable or those with obviously riveting narratives that begged for more elaboration.

After nearly an entire school year of reaching out to schools, listening to every word of every recording, and poring through transcripts, a structure began to emerge. And that's when we began to envision categories based on some common themes. Though none of them are rigid, and we argued internally about the placement of some students in one category over another, the labels became a more convenient way to talk about the nuance, intensity, and messiness in students' lives as we began to process what we had learned.

We know that Kentucky educators and policymakers are largely well-intentioned in their emphasis on college readiness. But all too often, the tendency in the research we read about college readiness is to depict students as abstractions. Relying heavily on statistics, many reports draw their conclusions largely from data points like these:

- In 2016, just one-fifth of Kentucky's 46,285 high school graduates taking the ACT met all the benchmark scores, showing they are ready for college-level coursework.[*]

- The percentage of graduates who were deemed college ready increased greatly between 2010 and 2012, but the percentage of graduates who enrolled in Kentucky colleges or universities the following year remained flat.[†]

- Of every one hundred ninth graders who enrolled in the 2008-2009 school year, just thirty-four persisted to a second year of college.[‡]

While such figures may give us an important academic foundation for understanding students' struggles, they tell us less about the other skills and behaviors that impact individual student success, many of which develop outside the classroom walls.

How can this type of expertise capture the reality of Lilian, who was diagnosed with a rare blood disorder, robbing her of the ability to recall information needed for tests, at the height of sophomore year? How can it explain the full triumph of Sal, who has conquered several rigorous Advanced Placement (AP) classes, despite living with the daily threat of his father's deportation? And how can such statistics ever get at the resilience of a student like Brianna, whose valiant efforts to pay the bills her parents have ignored for years are not reflected in her low ACT scores?

While value is rightly placed on quantitative data in education policymaking, the stories that bring them to life, often get pushed to the side, to the detriment of our understanding and our empathy.

Ready or Not is an attempt to shine a light on the stories behind the statistics.

By sharing what students have told us about their lives, we aspire to connect the head with the heart when thinking about public education policy. And in this case, specifically, we want to help humanize the postsecondary transition process.

We implore readers to follow the path we took, to listen to the voices we heard, and to come to understand—as we did—the profound value of student perspectives in making our schools better.

It is important to note how willing the students we interviewed were to open up to us. After just a few minutes of peer-facilitated conversation, many shared their heaviest burdens and lifetime struggles. And even more remarkable was the way student after student told us how talking with us marked the first time they felt as if their viewpoints about school even mattered.

That's how the students we spoke with became the Misnavigateds, the Givens, the Dismissers, the Moonlighters, the Newcomers, and the Oddsbuckers.

These are their stories.

Thank you for listening.

The Student Voice Team
Prichard Committee for Academic Excellence

Part One
The Misnavigateds

There are students nearing the end of high school who want to go to college but seem especially daunted by the process of getting there. Many seem to do well, or at least get by academically, with no obvious red flags on the way to high school graduation.

But they are the ones who may have no idea what college costs. Or they may be thwarted by the proper way to sign up for the ACT. Or they can't get their heads around which college offers the program that fits their interests and budget. And all too often, they don't know how to ask the right questions because the people who they look to for answers seem unable to advise them either correctly or at all.

They are the Misnavigateds.

Among other things, their stories highlight the critical nature of the teacher and student dynamic in the college preparation process, what happens when students don't have a person in their lives to push them, and the unintended barriers created by the ACT as a college admission test.

If there is a silver lining in this group, though, it may be that the Misnavigateds offer a place to invest limited resources. Though most of these students told us they have yet to even meet their school counselor, they are also the students for whom a little bit of good college guidance may make a major difference in a lifelong trajectory.

The Misnavigateds
Zach

"My dad keeps telling me that I'll know what I will want to do with my future when I feel it in my guts. My guts aren't telling me anything."

I think I want to be a teacher and a coach, so after I graduate, I've thought about studying education, business, sports management, or something like that. I am planning to go to college at a nearby state school. If college doesn't work out for some reason, and I drop out, I could always go back to the welding institute over here in town. I think I could figure something out.

I'm not too worried about the future, if you want me to be honest with you. If I get to go to college, that's great. If it doesn't happen, that's fine too. Either way or another, I'll be okay with what happens. I'll take any option. Do I prefer one or the other? No not really. I heard that college is very difficult, and I don't really want to put that much effort into it, especially when I don't get paid. I've been told that it could help me find a better job in the future, but I don't really want to think that far ahead. Plus, the welding institute here in town is super popular, and my parents don't really want me to leave or go too far away.

Both of my parents went to college, but neither of them finished. They told me that they were pretty smart when they were kids compared to their class, and I'm not. So if they can't do it, I doubt that I would be able to. I have two older siblings that went to college and finished though. My brother and sister are pushing me to do that too, but I can't forget all the hard times that they went through, and now, all the debt that they have stacked up. I don't want to follow their same path. If I go, my dad wants me to go into the Reserve Officer Training Corps (ROTC) because he puts pretty big emphasis on the military.

My dad keeps telling me that I'll know what I will want to do with my future when I feel it in my guts. He tells me that if I was cut out for the military, I would know it by now. I don't really know if I feel ready, so I'm probably not. My guts aren't telling me anything.

Right now I'm taking a small engine technician course, but the only thing I'm ever planning to do with lawnmowers is mow my yard. I'm spending this whole semester taking this course, but I don't need it at all. The guidance counselors put me in these classes I don't want, but I take them anyway. You know, like, if I didn't ever like college and dropped out, I could figure something else out like mowing lawns for a living. I mow my own lawn from time to time. I hate it. But you have to do what you need to do, and if I have to make a living off of it someday, so be it.

There are some classes that I wanted to take for enjoyment, something that I could have to look forward to every day. I got my first culinary class as a senior when I've been asking for it since freshman year. The counselors told me that it was because the class was limited and not everyone could have the opportunity, but my friends in the class told me that the teacher was complaining. She had never seen a class size so small, and it had made her worried. I don't know what's going on, and I never really asked any more questions.

I felt cheated, but I'm over it now. They don't really tell the students anything here anyway besides to pay attention, be quiet, and do our homework. You have to learn to take the blows just like every other student before you did. I'm not mad anymore. I'm not upset anymore. I am just a senior in a freshman cooking class.

My only traditional classes are English and College and Career Readiness. Everything else is electives like Business, Agriculture Sales, Agriculture, and Employability. I don't feel like I'm learning anything new at all. I sit in the classes and pay attention, but I feel like I'm learning the same information, just in different ways by different teachers. And worst of all, I still have no idea what that really means, "college ready." I mean, I spend almost every single day in a class dedicated to make me ready for college or a career, and the idea of the class is great, but we never actually do anything. At all. I just sit around and talk to my friends. It's a huge waste of time.

I'm pretty sociable. I have a close group of friends that I hang out with a lot, and if I could find friends like them in college, I know I will be fine socially. It might be academically and financially overwhelming though. I haven't prepared much, especially in the financial aspect. My grades are good, and I have passed most of my classes, so academically, I'm okay. I don't really take notes and don't take the classes I want though, so what's the point if I am getting an A in Agriculture when I want to study something else in college?

I did take AP Chemistry last year, which was hard. That was the only AP class I took, and it was the biggest mistake I made in my entire high school career. I didn't even end up taking the AP exam in the end because I knew that it would be a waste of my money. There was no way I was going to pass the test when I was barely even passing the class. Even though the class had the words "AP" in front of it, the way we worked in class was pretty similar to all the other classes I took. We still fooled around and talked to our friends for most of the class, and we almost never got any homework. The only difference was that the tests were a lot harder.

After that class, I officially gave up the idea of college being my only option. I considered the local community and technical college, but a teacher told me I'd be better off elsewhere. By elsewhere, I'm assuming he meant that I stay put in this county. Like me, most of my friends wanted to go to college, but they didn't prepare. Now we don't care anymore. It has worked out by itself so far. Why worry about it?

I don't think the ACT does a great job of showing college readiness, but I don't think GPA (Grade Point Average) does either. Some kids take easier classes than others, so their GPA might be higher with less work. For example, I worked way harder in AP Chem than any of my friends who just took Advanced Integrated Science. The two classes aren't even comparable. I barely passed my class while working a lot more than they did, but they still got higher grades and then a higher GPA. I bet you they just fooled around the entire time. The tests are probably over things they knew since sixth grade anyways.

At least I know that I am not college ready. A lot of people here at my school are worse off than I am, but they get an okay grade on the ACT and think that they are set and ready to go. No one in their families has ever even tried to go to college before, and they think that they are going to be the first ones to do it. Little do they know how hard it is going to be. They don't really know anything. They're going to get squashed.

The Misnavigateds
Emma

"We are captives in our culture."

We have an academic team, but nobody knows about it. Nobody, unless you're in game club or Future Business Leaders of America (FBLA), and there aren't that many people in my school that are necessarily proud to be in FBLA. It's not cool, like sports. The academic team has an amazing coach and knows more about any subject than most of the teachers combined. I bet you he could teach their classes better than the actual hired teachers would ever be able to. It is unfortunate that he's not very popular with the students because he "talks too much." I don't understand why kids get annoyed by his passion and intellect but not at jeering fans that repeat the same cheers and phrases at football games.

He talks too much about pushing people to college. He likes to tell students all there is to know about future opportunities, scholarships, and steps we can take to pursue a postsecondary education. I think the students are more distressed by the idea of their future than the teacher himself. They have misplaced anger because all of our futures are in disarray.

There are a lot of problems here at the high school. It would take me a fair share of time to explain them all. I'm not sure why I'd even bother telling you this. No one really wants to hear what the students have to say most times. Is any of this even going to matter?

For starters, we put all of our course emphasis on the AP program. More than eighty percent of the school's resources are funneled for those classes, which I find ironic. Students that are already succeeding past their grade level—a small portion of our student population—are receiving a majority of the funds, while those students who really need the attention and resources are nudged aside. We are convinced that we cannot reach heights outside of what our small town has to offer. It is normal to not ever leave the county, to get a job right after you graduate, to never leave home. I feel that this distortion of funding only encourages students to think this way and promotes this cycle of poverty.

We are captives in our culture.

I want to say that more than seventy-five percent of the student population is in the Future Farmers of America organization. One of their main events is to set aside an entire day in town for a tractor parade to promote the agriculture industry in the county. I mean come on. A tractor parade? Why don't we set aside days for an art show or some kind of big academic competition? I simply don't understand why we don't allow those things to be valued. Maybe we all do but are afraid to admit it. We don't want to be frowned upon as "that kid" that selfishly left their family for an overpriced education, one that won't even help the major manufacturing and agricultural jobs here.

I still want to go to college though. I'm planning on becoming a nurse practitioner. I'm already in a CNA (Certified Nursing Assistant) class now at the high school they offer. At the end of this semester, I will hopefully pass the test and get my nurse assistant license, and then for the rest of the year, I will work at the hospital or a nursing home. Right now, I know of another small town that is hiring nursing students, so I might be able to go there after school, but that's considering that nothing changes in the next few years. I doubt it will in towns like this, and I've seen my fair share of towns.

I was homeschooled until my freshman year when I moved here. My parents lived in Colorado and then moved to Michigan, where I was born. We moved from there to Arizona, Utah, Colorado—basically most of the continental US. I did most of my school work on the road.

It was on these road trips that I decided I wanted to be a nurse. As a kid, whenever a member of my family got sick, I was the go-to person. My five-year-old self would run around with a glass of water and Tylenol pills to my sick mom. I was always that person. For the last eighteen years of my life, I've taken care of my younger siblings before I thought of myself. My dad has never truly been a part of my life, and that leaves me and my mother to pay the bills and run the house.

I don't remember the last time I was young. I was dressing myself, feeding myself, and taking myself to school as early as elementary school. I've done more work around the house than I have homework. I am a mother, a caregiver in the home, before I am a student. I have to be. I have no other choice. I'm the glue. Without me, my family—what is left of it—would fall apart.

Over twenty different people have called me "glue." Every single time anybody needs anything health related or any mental support, they are redirected to me. I feel this innate need to go into nursing, to be a doctor or therapist. I mean, I feel like I'm programmed toward that because that is the role I have been assigned through my rough family life. Plus, there is the fact that everyone is always getting sick, and not just biologically.

On the surface, my high school persuades everyone to go to college and pursue an education, but most teachers don't give a crap about the students. There are like one or two teachers here that really, really, really try, like my medical teacher who pushes us and is genuinely passionate about what she does. She's the one that pushes us to do well because she's the only teacher of mine that's ever cared. All the rest of them are like, "Here are some papers. Fill them out and pass my class so that I can get rid of you."

They don't care if we go to college, the workforce, or even drop out of high school to have more time to waste on drugs, so they prepare us for nothing. You know a college is supposed to be like a lecture, and the students take notes based on the lectures and everything. That's how it's supposed to be. Most of my teachers use the excuse that the "system" limits what they can teach, but I know that's not true. I've looked them up. The standards so far have been guidelines, not finite steps that must be taken. But the teachers don't work on anything by themselves based on what the students need. They just get a book from "the people above" and feed it to us, and that's it. I went up to my teacher today before this interview and told her that I didn't understand a concept, and that I knew I would miss it on the test if it came up. She barely gave me a sideways glance and told me that she didn't have any justification in what her authorities mandate I learn. I would google the answer, but I don't have internet at home.

This is the reason we act the way we do. Not to say that students don't make mistakes either, but this is why we don't see so many students do well in school. So many brilliant minds here go to waste. When I wash the dishes at home, my younger siblings sometimes don't eat their vegetables. The food, the best thing for our bodies, is just wasted and left to rot in the trash—no different than underappreciated students.

Here we keep our students confined to the same regimented schedule, and we keep teaching them the same stuff they learned in sixth grade. My senior classes are almost no different than what I have been introduced to in middle school. Nothing that we learn is relevant to our culture. Like, do I need to learn the quadratic equation to get from the gas station to my home? No, you really don't. To add up my income and subtract my debt for the bills? To pay my taxes? To take care of my younger siblings? To make sure that there is food on the table? I don't need the quadratic equation when I know that I am going to be stuck in this county for my entire life.

I want to get out and practice medicine, but a part of me knows that's never going to happen. Nothing I have done so far has prepared me for college. No, not even the ACT. I hate the ACT. The ACT covers the four subjects, and the science section doesn't even have any science on it. It's just so you know how to read graphs. I'm on the roll to take the ACT for my seventh time. Every time I've taken the science portion, there's no actual science on it. There is nothing that aligns with my classes.

I've taken it so many times because I haven't even met the benchmark. I got an eighteen and can't get any higher. Every single time I take it, my English and reading scores are both around a thirty, but then my math hovers around a twelve or thirteen. I don't understand the process, and I doubt I ever will. When I was homeschooled, I would get these books that taught me long division, interest equations, and percentage proportions—useful math. I learned and retained them because I actually used them in my daily life. It was real to me. This test doesn't measure how college ready I am at all because it measures skills only they think are valuable for college success, when in reality, no one really knows.

Personally, I could have entered college as a high school freshman. I took the IQ test my freshman year, and I was 130, classified as a genius. I took it just a couple of weeks ago, and I was still a 125. I know how to live on my own, and most importantly, I don't give up. If I have trouble with a topic, I will figure it out, whether it be talking to my teachers or learning it on my own. I might not value the information, but I know it is important.

If I can somehow manage to run my entire house and get a high GPA, I know that I could do anything. Anything except afford college. No one wants to help out a girl that can't even meet benchmarks. They don't care about anything they can't measure, and they definitely don't like vegetables.

The Misnavigateds
Tabitha

"I mean, I have my FAFSA and that's all I need. FAFSA will cover everything, right? It can't be that expensive. A semester in college can't be more than like—I don't know. A thousand dollars?"

It's my first year at this new high school. I don't really talk much. I'm willing to bet you my paycheck that after seven months, the teachers don't know my name. I guess it all works out in the end. The teachers never really want to talk to me either.

On a normal day, I walk in, I get handed papers and worksheets that I need to fill out. The teacher sits behind their desk, and the class fools around and plays on their phones. On tests, well if you even want to count them as tests, kids don't even try to hide their phones. Why should we go through all the trouble and try to be secretive when we know we won't get punished? We just tell the answers to each other because we didn't even do the classwork. There isn't a point to that either. We don't check classwork or go over it, and when we do, we don't understand it. Why waste all the time filling out the stupid things when we are just going to pass the tests anyway?

I haven't been here long, but I guess it's okay. Everyone is nice and seems friendly. It is kinda weird. All the kids here are used to the teachers and the way things work, but I guess I have a new view on things. I see things in a different way than everyone who has lived here for a while does. And to me, everything is superficial.

Like I said, everyone is nice. They smile at lunch and the teachers welcome you to class, but I don't really talk to anyone, haven't brought a friend home yet, haven't had a meaningful conversation with a teacher, and it's almost been a year. I know I'm quiet, but I haven't changed since I was at my last school, and things were different there. Maybe it is because the school doesn't take us seriously. We are just another face, another student that they have to get through the system. They have to teach us to jump through the obstacles like trained dogs or something. They don't see us as people. I've never had this kind of discussion with anyone, and I've only been speaking to you for two minutes.

None of my teachers are amazing or terrible. They are just there. They are present, and that is all there is to it. I never go home and tell my parents about something that happened at school because there is nothing to tell. No stories about the mean teacher that gave us a pop quiz or a really hard test. No stories about something really cool that I learned in class. It's all dull. Students think so; teachers think so. It's not hard to tell that we've all had enough. I haven't even been here for a year, and I've had enough.

There's been like a whole bunch of drama already. I didn't really start dating 'til like my freshman year of high school, and it's been trouble. I decided I didn't want to get involved too much with anyone at the new school and instead, found a guy I really like and have been with him for almost the entire year. But a couple of other boys kept bothering me. I told them that I didn't want to be with them, that I had moved on, and it was over. I was with someone else anyway. But they were in my homeroom and wouldn't stop. The teacher didn't say anything even when they kept screaming and poking at me. I didn't really say anything until one day at lunch.

When you're on the Free or Reduced Lunch Program, you get to come to school a little early and get breakfast before class starts. Some people use it as an excuse to see their friends, but others really need the food. They don't have anything at home. Monday mornings are the most crowded because some kids are starving from the weekend. The guy that was bothering me actually came up to me one day at breakfast and like hit me on the back of the head. I was caught off guard, it was out of nowhere.

I kinda just like—I kinda snapped on him a little bit. I like screamed at him and the whole cafeteria shut up real quick. Like literally, it all went quiet, and then I just went over and told the principal. I had to tell someone besides my teachers because I had finally had enough of his behavior. I told him everything: how this should be called out as abuse, both verbal and physical, how he hit me in the middle of the cafeteria where everyone saw, how I yelled at him, and how he laughed. How all the students around me didn't say a word. How the teachers pretended not to notice. How the cafeteria ladies pretended that nothing in the world was wrong.

He said that these things happen all the time. That this wasn't the first situation like this. That I need to stand up for myself and not let things like this get out of hand. He told me that he'd take care of it this time since it was my first complaint.

It's called the trailer. If you get in trouble, it's like you go out back outside the school building and stay there for detention, or something like that. I've never been—only heard of it. The guy that hit me went back out there, and then he hasn't emailed me for a while. Then he started emailing me and asking me questions, and I don't respond even though I see him in school all the time. It's the main reason I don't really like school anymore, why I'm okay with missing a few classes because it means that I will feel safer. I don't care if my grades suffer or if I won't be able to get into college.

My parents know what has been going on, I mean to an extent. I'm not living with them anymore. I'm actually living with my boyfriend. Me and him were on the phone with my parents not too long ago. They told me to just talk to the principal and have it handled, but I knew that wasn't going to do anything. And plus, my parents don't really know too much about my life anymore. It's nice that they want to help, but I don't think they really know how or give the best advice. We still talk a lot though and see each other almost every week.

My boyfriend, though, he doesn't want me to drop out. I've told him that was something I was thinking about, but he's actually pushing me to go to school. He is pushing me to do what I want to do in life. But, I mean, that is just what he says. Those are just words. He actually lets me do what I kinda want. In a way, it's just like the school teachers. They tell me that they want the best for me, that they'll take care of me, that they will help me get where I want to go, but they are just words. They don't really do anything to prove what they say.

After I graduate I'm wanting to go to local community and technical college to get my associates degree, and then, hopefully, I will go to a four-year university. I want to become a teacher in the end. Not because I have loved my teachers and that they have inspired me, but because I know I can do such a better job. They're getting paid to do nothing but hand us papers and occasionally grade them. I hope I get to work with younger kids. I have two half-sisters and a full blood brother. I'm not really close with any of them really, but we get along, and I'm sure I could do the same with little kids.

One of my half-siblings is older than me though. She tried going to college, but then she like dropped out. She wants to go back, but I don't ever think she will. She's been saying the same things for a couple of months, but like my boyfriend, like my teachers, like the school, doesn't do anything about it. Man, I really hate words.

I know that in order to get there I have to take the ACT and stuff, so I took it last year. I met benchmarks in math and science, but not in English and reading. I could take it again, but that is going to take a lot of effort, and a lot of money, so I don't think I will. In December I will take the Kentucky Online Test (KYOTE) which is something like the ACT but easier, and if I pass it, then the school will call me college ready, and I don't need to sit through that long ACT ever again.

I think that once I meet benchmarks though, I will really be college and career ready. I mean, that is what the entire test is made for right? I'm not really sure where I want to go, how to apply, or even how to pay for it. I don't know if I even want to leave my boyfriend. But when I get college ready, I think I can figure it out, right? When I actually pass the KYOTE, I won't be worried about college as much because I know that the school thinks I'm smart enough. I mean, I have my FAFSA (Free Application for Federal Student Aid) and that's all I need. FAFSA will cover everything, right? It can't be that expensive. A semester in college can't be more than like—

I don't know?

A thousand dollars?

Whatever happens, I know that if I don't go to college, I can still end up like my parents and my boyfriend. I'll get used to saying things and not doing stuff about it. Right now, I don't know if college is right for me. I don't think I'll go down that path.

The Misnavigateds
Tyler

"I hope that before graduation, I can finish an application and get accepted in a college. Is second semester senior year too late?"

I was cheated by my school.

Well, that may be a little extreme, but it sure feels that way. Like, every single day in class, I am being told by all of my teachers that I have to meet their stupid deadlines, that they set without even asking us, but I meet them anyway I guess. But then, the one time that I need something that is actually important, the school itself misses all the deadlines. Our school can be last minute about stuff. Very last minute, and I'm not sure why.

I think it could be because of the bad wifi, and that could make communication difficult in the school. Like the wifi just shuts out, and I don't know if it's because of that. It is not weird for the school to have no internet access at all for three of the five school days out of the week, and sometimes, it will go out for weeks at a time. On the days where we do have it though, it keeps going on and off every ten to fifteen minutes, so it's, like, impossible to get any work done. It's whatever, I guess. The teachers and administration don't really seems to care about it anymore, and they don't get it fixed nearly as fast as they used to, so why should I care, right?

But I don't care how or why the school misses deadlines. I usually never care too much about anything in school. I'm a go-with-the-flow kind of guy, you know? This time though, I was just so mad. I was cheated. That was a few weeks ago, and I'm over it now. There really is no point in being mad or angry about something that I can't fix. What am I going to do? Talk to a teacher about it? Talk to a counselor? Who even is my counselor? Do you really think that they will do anything to fix it when they are the ones that created the problem in the first place? No, so don't worry about it. Don't waste your energy. It's whatever.

See, on that Saturday, the majority of the seniors were going to retake the ACT. All of us had already taken the state mandated one, or whatever that was, and this was our second shot. The school really wanted us to do well and helped us take the ACT again to raise our scores.

But they did something really weird.

At first it sounded like a good idea. It made sense why they were doing what they were. A few weeks before the test date, all the seniors were split into, I think, two groups. So half of the kids are in one group, and half were in the other. It was pretty obvious that one of the groups had higher scores than the other group. Like, all the smart kids that always did well in class were placed together and separated. I was not part of that group.

They told us that the groups were created so that we could have special ACT tutoring classes that could best suit our needs. Like, the people that did better would need to focus more on testing strategies and the little things to get a higher score, while kids like me would have classes that would focus on the actual content. They would also give us practice materials and stuff there too. It seemed like a really good idea. They didn't have enough staff to teach both groups at once, so they split us up.

The smart people took ACT prep courses two weeks before the test, and we took them the week before. Like, the school days before that Saturday. Like, just a few days before one of the biggest tests of our lives. Even if we wanted to, and most of us didn't, honestly, we wouldn't have time like the other group to study. I thought it was weird how they planned that. Why wait so long, you know?

Then they told us we had to renew our picture for the ACT, and if we didn't renew it, we couldn't take the ACT. So some of the seniors couldn't take the ACT because they didn't hear about that. You know what though? Almost all of the kids in the first group knew that they had to change their pictures. Almost all of the kids in my group didn't. It's not that we didn't want to this time. We literally did not know. The kids that did change their pictures did it because they heard it from their friends in the other group, but I don't really hang with them. My picture stayed the same. I didn't take the ACT again. It's whatever.

Some of my friends think that the school did it on purpose. Like, they made sure that all the smart people with the higher scores were able to take it again because they had a better chance of improving or getting into college, and we didn't. They think that it was all staged and we were cheated because the school wanted to make it seem as if their scores are higher. I don't know what to believe. It doesn't seem like a crazy idea though. Wouldn't surprise me if it were true.

Anyway, I feel like I did better on the December ACT than the one I took last year. I was able to score a fifteen. I will take it again if I'm not happy with my score, but I think my second semester of senior year is too late. I don't really know how to be college ready. The ACT is just like a filter test. It's like, "If you score this high, these are the colleges you can go to." I don't really know how to prepare myself for something like that.

One of the college prep people at my school told me that the ACT is like nothing. Because, let's say you score a twenty-five. You score a twenty-five, you're able to go to Northern Kentucky University (NKU), but you have to be accepted first. So just because you can go to NKU doesn't mean you are accepted. So the ACT, I don't really know its purpose, other than to try and get a high score on it. But other than that, if you score a low score, then you try again.

I hope that before graduation, I can finish an application and get accepted in a college. I'm going to be working on my NKU application, and then I will work on other college applications. Hopefully, I'll start them soon. Is second semester senior year too late? Would you know?

I hope after summer, around fall, that I'm already in college. I don't care where, just anywhere. I'm going to be working on a bachelor's degree. I like physics, but I want to be in athletics. I run track and I have played football for four years, but I think track is more my thing than football. My school system has this thing where if you were here from Kindergarten to now without moving at all, you get some sort of scholarship, and you get to go somewhere for free. Ms. W, I think she is one of our counselors, told me about it, and that got me really excited. It turns out that it's true, so I hope to get some money from there.

Every last one of our teachers want us to be college and/or career ready. Like every last one of them. I mean, they bug us about it everyday. They really want us to achieve those goals. I'm pretty sure though if someone says they're not going to go to college, they aren't going to say anything. It is a normal thing around here. But then they will say, "Okay, you should be career ready instead." I mean, they're trying. But some people just don't care. Sometimes it's not actually the school's fault, even though I feel cheated sometimes. Sometimes it's the people we go to school with, the students. Sometimes it is just where we are in the state and the money we have. Sometimes it is just that things won't change, so we need to get used to them.

Some just don't care. They want to do their own thing. They are just there because they have to be there. I don't like being around people like that; they're annoying. They ruin it for the whole class and for the teacher. They argue.

There is always at least one argument per day. At least one. The mindset of some of the people I have to deal with at school is just done. I have really had enough. They think that they're always right, and if they aren't right, then you must be wrong. They will even fight to prove that you're wrong when you obviously know that you're right. The things I have to deal with is annoying. Freshman year was okay. Sophomore year was annoying. Junior year was just irritating. Now senior year, it's plain annoying. Now, if it happens, it's just whatever. You never really get used to it, it's annoying. But if it happens, it's just whatever.

It happens, and you move on.

You can't just think about it. You cannot think about how the other schools across the county lines are so much better than us. Sure they have more money than us, so they're going to have better equipment and teachers and stuff. That is what happens when you have money. But we can be just as good, if not better than them, if we try.

Too bad everyone here is dumb. They'd rather be lazy. They would rather stay up at night. They would rather smoke weed. They would rather drink and stuff. They would rather move on from their dreams and future.

They move on.

Part Two
The Givens

In every high school we have visited, including our own, we have noticed students whom administrators and teachers seem proud to showcase as proof that the system works.

Some were identified early as academically advanced. Others may not have always performed perfectly grade-wise, but they have always seemed invested in school and known the next step. Whatever college these students aspired to after high school, no matter the cost or the inconvenience, they felt assured they would and could figure out how to get there. For these select students, and from early on, college has never been a question of if, but rather, simply, a matter of where.

They are the Givens.

These are the students who stand on a foundation of certainty. They trust not only that they can find the funds to afford college, but also that they will be supported to and through it.

The forces propelling these students to postsecondary education are varied. It could be parents, teachers, counselors, peers, communities, or some combination, so long as it affirms that college is critical and non-negotiable.

But even some of these students face challenges in persisting to a college degree. They may wrestle with mental health issues like anxiety, sleep and eating disorders, or early burn out, all too often masked by high test scores, remarkable grades, or material privilege.

The Givens remind us that even if we realize everything high schools do to prepare students academically, we should challenge the notion of whether that alone equates to college readiness.

The Givens

Ajay

"To prepare myself for the rigorous course load in college and to be a more competitive applicant, I will have taken a total of seventeen AP and dual credit courses by the end of my senior year. This is not unusual at my school."

It is imperative to review my past and the legacy I follow to fully understand my perceptions on my future educational goals. To fight the encroaching Japanese empire, my great grandfather had to leave his pregnant wife and five children in their small town in British-occupied Kerala, India. While he came back alive from the greatest power struggle known to man, he did not survive too long after his homecoming. Again, he left his family, but this time he left my grandfather, the eldest of six children, to take care of the family. Sunny, my grandfather, was still in high school when he had to drop out and start working at the age of sixteen to support his mother, who, as a woman in those times, was discouraged from working, and his five younger siblings.

For the remainder of his working career, he slaved away in steel plants that produced railways from one Indian province to the next, earning deplorable wages. But this time, he had a family of his own to provide for. He had a wife, a son, and a daughter, all of whom would have to live in poverty. While my mother was at the top of her class and dreamed of becoming a doctor, the education system in India was, and still is, rigged against the poor, no matter how brilliant. Thus, not having the necessary resources to pay her way through the entrance examinations and medical school, she could not follow her lifelong dreams.

Since then, my mother instilled the importance of education in me from a very young age. She believed that the reason why my grandfather worked a poor paying job was because he did not finish his educational pursuits, in effect, not allowing herself to pursue her educational goals either. I believe strongly that education is the key not only to make a better living, but is also a remedy to the vast majority of social ills in the long term. Thus, I plan on attending college and majoring in political science and international studies.

To prepare myself for the rigorous course load in college and to be a more competitive applicant, I will have taken a total of seventeen AP and dual credit courses by the end of my senior year. This is not unusual at my school; in fact, many other students share similar rigorous course loads, and it is expected of us as students at my high school to take challenging courses. In addition to a burdensome schedule, we are encouraged to participate in several extracurricular activities. I have participated in thirteen after-school activities and summer programs. Some of these activities are the debate team, Beta Club, Young Democrats, and the Benjamin Franklin Transatlantic Fellows. However, a common occurrence here, and at many other schools too, is that several students will participate in "fluff" extracurriculars in which they need to do very little and will still receive an officer's position. While these clubs contribute very little authenticity to college applications, the mindset of students is that if there are not enough activities to fully fill the form, then it will make them look uncompetitive. I cannot evaluate the validity of this statement, but I will say, in a very cliché manner, that you should do what you love and follow it through.

I have been and will be at this school for the entirety of my high school career, and I believe that it's the best fit for me and other like-minded individuals. This is because everyone who attends this school has to apply to one of our five magnet programs: Visual Arts; High School University; Math, Science, and Technology; Youth Performing Arts School; or Journalism and Communications. Nationally recognized, all five magnets are highly reputable and highly decorated programs. This is in part due to dedicated teachers in each magnet who strive to fulfill every student's educational endeavors. The environment that is fostered at my school, however, is sadly unique and cannot be found in other high schools in the district or beyond. This is primarily the reason why the graduating class of 2015 received over sixty-six million dollars of scholarship money.

Since everyone is expected to attend college from this school, it is a constant topic of discussion and debate. I would say that my friends have greatly influenced where I am looking at for college. For the longest time, I was not looking at California schools, but a couple of my close friends, who graduated last year, are now attending these schools and absolutely love them. Probably by the mere-exposure effect, I am loving them too. I will now definitely apply to colleges like USC (University of Southern California), UCLA (University of California, Los Angeles), and Stanford.

Just as how college is a hot topic at this school, so are standardized tests, the ACT especially. I have taken the infamous ACT twice this year, and I will take it again. While the ACT and other standardized tests are prominent in the college admission process, I doubt their ability to gauge college readiness. Several prominent research studies have shown that the ACT only measures socioeconomic status and not content knowledge or college readiness. The design of the ACT does not test for content knowledge but rather how well you can take the test. Thus, the only way to score well on the ACT is access to test prep resources. This is extremely troubling when considering that inner city public schools, with the majority of students being minorities, are disadvantaged from being competitive in the college admission process against wealthier private school students.

Even though the ACT has flaws in gauging the ability of students to perform well in postsecondary education, it is a standard and objective way of measuring a student's ability. A world without the ACT and no other procedures to replace it has the potential to become even more subjective because other factors will be weighed more heavily. For example, a student's extracurricular activities might be weighed more heavily, but this might create more inequality because some wealthier schools have a plurality of clubs while others do not. In essence, there is no method currently known to me that controls for socioeconomic factors that objectively evaluates a student's ability to perform in college.

However, even thinking about going to college is a privilege because many students do not possess the financial resources to receive their postsecondary education. How much a college offers me in scholarships is my primary deciding factor for which university I would want to attend. I want to graduate with my bachelor's degree with under five thousand dollars in debt because I know that my grad school debts will be astronomically high, and I want to save my money for that expense. This October when I am applying for colleges, I will also fill out the FAFSA. To be honest, I am not too familiar with the procedures that I will have to follow when I do apply for the FAFSA, but I will know by October! In addition to the FAFSA, I will apply for other scholarship opportunities. However, I am not aware of all the options I have and when I have to submit different applications. A step that can be taken to make financial aid more feasible is for all the scholarship and college information to be on one website run by a reputable organization or the government.

My main source of information about the college application process and scholarship opportunities is my counselor. However, neither me nor my counselor have the time to meet each other every time I have a question about college. She has around 500 other students to aid, more than two thousand students for four counselors. I do know my counselor better than my fellow classmates, though, because I have been meeting with her pretty regularly throughout the school year. But this is the first year I am meeting with her and discussing my plans for college.

In the end, there are many purposes for high school, with college being one of the major ones, but it is important to remember to always keep above the flack of unhealthy competition and to try your best.

The Givens
Blair

"I have always achieved because I have used every resource available to me. I know that I probably have a lot more than most people at my disposal."

When it comes to school, I have always had every advantage.

I have gone to private schools since kindergarten. I have always been one of those "smart kids" that everyone else hates. My brain is wired to learn, and I embrace this passionately.

Now, in high school, I am one of the twenty-one girls in the top ten percent of my grade. I am required to take all honors classes and four AP classes by the time I graduate. However, I have already taken six at the end of my junior year. I push myself at all times; my classes challenge me, but I also challenge myself outside of the classroom. I attend church every single Sunday. I am a part of twenty-five clubs and extracurriculars, and my freshman and sophomore year, I played lacrosse. Unfortunately, I took four AP classes this year, and my schedule no longer permitted me to play lacrosse.

I know I am only this successful because my life circumstance allows it. I can receive help in any subject of school or any aspect of my life with which I need assistance. I always have been able to. At my high school, I have a guidance counselor who is a true and caring friend to me. I have a college counselor who I am well acquainted with, an advanced program director who I can always turn to with problems, an academic dean, and I have the help of any of the faculty or teachers in my school at my disposal. My school has two college counselors, four guidance counselors (one per grade), a post-secondary planning program with two full-time teachers for students with academic disabilities or learning differences, an advanced program with a director, and two academic deans. All of these aforementioned faculty and staff want all of the students at our school to succeed, they want us to push ourselves to the limit without falling overboard, and they care about us as people.

That is one giant difference between my school and any other. The thing that sets us apart from most other schools is that the school is a community. We all care for one another. Here you do not just receive an academic education, but you are taught how to be a good citizen and person. The focus is not only on developing you as a student, but as a person. And the community surrounding you has your back, always.

I have always achieved because I have used every resource available to me. I know that I probably have a lot more than most people at my disposal, but I never let one go down the drain.

One unfair advantage that I know I have, and have always had, is money. My family is not a family of billionaires, but we are smart with our money and never have to worry about food or electricity. Even when my mother was diagnosed with stage four lung cancer, money was never an issue. This can easily translate into tutoring. I can pay someone to tutor me if I need to. So, when I needed an ACT tutor, I got one, no questions asked. As I began seeing this tutor, I began to think about how unfair it truly was that I was allowed this opportunity. I eventually was able to raise my ACT four points to a thirty-two with the help of this tutor. I know my score before, a twenty-eight, was not bad at all, but I wanted to have a more competitive score. So, I paid my way into it.

No, I didn't cheat and pay someone else to take the test for me, but I paid a man to teach me math specifically for the ACT, and I can see that it made a difference. My ACT math went from a twenty-four to a thirty between one test. I paid for a better score, and I am lucky that I can. My money helped me to become smarter, but some people cannot pay for ACT tutoring, let alone food. This is why I very strongly believe that the ACT is not an accurate representation of college readiness.

One other thing that most college administrations do not tend to take into account is life circumstances. During the end of my sophomore year, my mother was diagnosed. This had a very adverse effect on my grades. Although not major, I had received two B's; these two B's were the first I had ever been assigned. During this time, I also hosted a South African exchange student for a month. My life was everywhere and my thoughts had never been messier or more complicated. My mother's battle had little effect on my schoolwork because it became a priority to do most of my work to my best ability, even when I was sitting in a hospital room to complete it.

Once my mother died at the beginning of my junior year, my life became even messier; focusing my energy on schoolwork became the only way I could forget it. I knew I could get through it because I had a support system of family, friends, and schoolmates. My entire school united behind me. For some, they are not as lucky. Their problems are not seen as catastrophic or detrimental to them. Sometimes their problems do not seem like a problem to the school board. Some have no one to help them when they have no food in their house, or when they have to work two jobs and complete school work after going to school all day. I am lucky. I am blessed to have a support network.

The Givens
Matt

"I can't say enough about how tremendous my counselors have been and stuff. If they weren't there, then I would have struggled a bit, and it would have taken longer."

A lot of kids at my school play sports. About half of them do. Almost all of school funding just goes to sports. Every single time I see fundraising at the school, it always pays for football or soccer. We don't live without our sports. A lot more people fundraise for sports, and then the arts program and the theater program kinda get left behind, but we don't have a lot of theater stuff. We have a play once a year and a lot of people go to that but don't sign up for it. The arts program, it's kinda like neutral. They are maintained, and they still make enough money to fund it and everything, so it's kinda evened out. It will float for a little while longer.

It's good that I don't really care for the arts that much. Like, yeah, they're important, but they're not my main focus. Luckily, I'm really involved with sports here. They get a lot of hype, and anyone that really wants any attention at the school, by students or teachers, needs to be involved in sports. Other than athletics, I'm taking a couple of AP classes and multiple college classes. I'm taking AP Environmental Science, and then I'll be taking the college math off campus. I'm doing an online class for the first semester of my history class, then for the second semester, I'm doing arts and humanities. I'm just taking it to graduate and get all the credits I need. Otherwise, those classes are a big joke. We don't learn anything, and I'm pretty sure that the teachers don't know what they are talking about all the time either. I'm just going to get it over with.

I've got everything planned out. I've been accepted, and I'm going to the local community and technical college. I don't know my major yet, but I'm going to try and transfer to the university afterwards. There's a plan at the community college where if you go there and then transfer to a university, you pay the same amount of money you did at the college for the classes.

Our college and career ready guidance counselor told us that. She has these weeks set up for us. Like this week, Monday was all about scholarships. Tuesday was applications. Yesterday was money, money, money, and all that. Most of her days are focused on just applications for the students, and she's really good about setting up stuff, but sometimes, she will be busy and sometimes has so much on her plate and forgets that she has an appointment with you. I feel kinda bad for her. She tries so hard to do her best for every single student, but sometimes, there are just too many of us. I think that she sees about two hundred students? I'm not sure, but it is something crazy like that. A lot of people do go to her for college stuff. She's the main counselor at our school, like the president of all the college stuff. We do have two more people, our actual guidance counselor and there's another one, but I forgot what he is. They are good with college stuff too. We've been meeting with them since freshman year, but no one is as amazing as the chief.

If it wasn't for her, I wouldn't be going to college, and I wouldn't be able to afford it. I know that. I can't say enough about how tremendous my counselors have been and stuff, but if they weren't there, then I would have struggled a bit, and it would have taken longer. I'll be the first one in my family to go to college. I know I wouldn't be able to say that if it wasn't for my counselor.

Freshman year, we mainly focused on our GPAs. She told us at the beginning you "wanna" focus mainly on your GPA because that's where you all start off at. If you start off bad, you have to get it up over four years, but if you start off good, you can "kinda" take a little weight off your shoulders. She explained to us how all of our grades really mattered, and that it was important for us to realize that. No one else really bothered giving us the "why" explanation behind it. I mean, yeah, teachers wanted us to get good grades, but they never really get through to the kids who don't want to study and don't care. She did, because she treated us like responsible adults who could handle the full explanation.

I'd say I'm going to be getting fifteen hundred to seventeen hundred dollars in KEES (Kentucky Educational Excellence Scholarship) for the first four years. I'm looking mainly on the scholarship. I was going to go play baseball, but the right college is never calling me that I want. They're all like, "You know how the DIII (National College Athletic Association Division III) is set up and how they can't give you any scholarships." They were all too expensive. The university is twenty-six thousand dollars to go there a year. I can save thirteen thousand dollars of it since I'll be going to the community college for thirteen thousand dollars a year. A lot of people don't know about this program, and I think that it is hurting them. Many people look at the community college like it is a bad thing. They either don't go to college at all or force themselves to go to the huge state school that costs a lot more. They are screwing themselves over because I am getting the same education, just half the price.

I filled out my FAFSA, but it doesn't help. My dad is a plant manager at three different plants in three different states. He didn't need college to do all of this work, so for a while, it was hard for me to realize that I actually needed college to be able to do well in life. Just look at my parents. They didn't really have any type of postsecondary education, but they were living comfortably. What was the point?

My parents are strict on college because they want the absolute best for me and want to give me more than they ever had. They've helped me so much, and they support me and continue to support me. When I decided not to play college baseball, they weren't okay with it at first. But then they realized it's not what I want to get up every day and do, and they have started to support me. I think that they are just glad that I am taking the extra step that they didn't. It's a little hard for me because I have to figure everything out on my own, but I think I can do it.

I've taken the ACT four times. I took it just last weekend. I really hate long tests, I hate them so much. On the ACT, I get the same score every single time. I'm not afraid to say I got a nineteen, so I'm not really good at it. The weird thing is I'll do really good on one subject on one test, and I'll benchmark in all three things that I needed to get to college, so I don't have to take any remedial classes, but I haven't been able to get a good score on all three of them combined in one test.

The college and career readiness counselor gave me an ACT booklet with the answers and everything, and I practiced that, then I came to the library over here and looked at a few books and was able to study them. There's shortcuts that they taught me, and I found some shortcuts on the ACT too, but the ACT is literally one test, and it determines your whole entire college career. I think the GPA means a whole lot more because it shows how hard you work from your first year all the way to your senior year. I think a GPA shows more than an ACT. A kid I played baseball with has a 4.0 but only got an eighteen on the ACT because he is horrible at long tests, and he doesn't have a benchmark in math right now.

In the end, I feel more prepared than some students I know that got crazy high scores like twenty-fives or twenty-sixes. I know I'm going to college. I don't have to waste money on remedial courses, (even if I met the benchmarks by one or two points), and I know that I will find adults that can help me through the entire process. I have done a lot of planning with my counselor, and even though my ACT score may not be the best, it is just one part of me. Some kids, I think, get so caught up on the test that they forget about everything else, and that is where things really start falling apart.

I think taking college classes in high school helps because they show what you have to do and what all you are doing, like all the work they're giving you and how you're reacting to it, how to manage your time because college is a lot about time management. It is a lot because you've got papers due. You've got tests to study for. High school is literally all babying, but come to college, and they throw you out in the world. I'm not sure if I'm ready to be thrown out yet, but I know I'm more prepared than a lot of people from my county. If not me, then who?

The Givens
Alice

"We watch the same, cheesy, cringe-worthy suicide prevention video at the beginning of every year, and that's where discussion of mental health ends."

I'm a sophomore, and I've lived in this city since I moved here from Boston thirteen years ago. I've always attended public school, and I plan to attend my high school for all four years.

I love my school. It is a magnet school, meaning it unites students who each focus on a different subject or skill, such as performing arts, visual art, or math, science, and technology. This creates a unique environment in which I'm exposed to many perspectives and am able to meet diverse peers. I've found that after only a couple years here, my friends have changed the way I think and allowed me to consider new ideas with an open mind. I am driven by this motivated and varied student body. We have many student-run clubs and after-school activities ranging from Science Olympiad to environmental initiatives.

I'm fortunate enough to attend a school where there's not much to improve upon in terms of opportunities. But there's another critical issue that few seem to talk about—mental health disorders. While it's great that we offer almost every AP class there is and that we always are pushed to challenge ourselves, there's not a student at my school who isn't consistently stressed and sleep deprived. However, even though mental health challenges are certainly not restricted to just my school, administrators on all levels aren't doing much to tackle this looming issue. We watch the same, cheesy, cringe-worthy suicide prevention video at the beginning of every year, and that's where discussion of mental health ends. With no valuable education about the causes of mental health disorders, students are often forced to try to work out these issues alone.

Mental health is an issue that needs to be addressed. I'm glad to see students beginning to take more initiatives to address psychological wellness—some of my peers recently founded a mental health advocacy group that works to decrease the stigma surrounding mental illness. However, students alone cannot tackle this problem. For example, it won't take much for teachers or administrators to incorporate mental health education into health class or homeroom.

To me, the purpose of postsecondary education is twofold. First, this provides a valuable transition period for students to get a taste of freedom and maturity before full-fledged adulthood. Second, I think college gives students many unique opportunities to explore many interests and broaden their education. College is important and beneficial for some, but it doesn't necessarily fit everyone's needs. Vocational paths, while often stigmatized, are still a useful way for people to successfully enter the workforce.

Though my mom was a young refugee when she came to this country, and my paternal grandparents immigrated from Vietnam as teenagers, both of my parents are fluent English speakers, went to college, and obtained medical degrees. My family has always motivated me to go to college. I think they believe that a college education is necessary for success, though I don't think that's true in every case. However, I think college would fit my personal needs, and I plan to attend postsecondary education.

Most of my friends are also planning to go to college. My friends are planning to apply to many different places, but I simply hope to attend a college that fits my personal needs and interests, and I hope my friends do as well. My peers and I don't really actively encourage each other to go to college, but it's pretty much implied at my school—ninety-eight percent of our students attend postsecondary education after graduation. Teachers and counselors both encourage us to attend college, and help us find opportunities, build skills to write application essays, and compile lists of scholarships to apply to.

Our counselors are particularly involved in the application process. Our guidance office has a college and career center, where you can learn more about applications and particular schools. Counselors write recommendations for every student and are always open to having one-on-one discussions about college. However, we only have four counselors for our two thousand students, so most students don't get to know their counselor very well.

I'm lucky to attend a school that's very focused on giving students a challenging, thorough education. I take several AP classes, and our school offers almost every class that exists. I've decided to take AP classes for the academic challenge and because of the potential for college credit. I participate in and have leadership positions in several extracurriculars, including Science Olympiad and Science Bowl, Women in Science and Engineering, and Speak Out, my school's mental health advocacy group. So far, I think I'm a relatively good student. I've earned straight A's my whole life, and I try to challenge myself academically inside and outside of school. However, while I've gained the necessary maturity and responsibility for college from other life challenges, I don't think my academic skills alone are a good description of college readiness.

The ACT is constantly repeated as the gold standard of college readiness. I have not taken the official ACT before, but I have taken school-sponsored practice exams. I'm planning on taking it at the beginning and end of my junior year. While the ACT has some value, it should not be the be all end-all of college readiness. It may show, in a limited sense, academic readiness for college, but does not reflect maturity or responsibility. Unfortunately, the ACT is unfairly skewed towards those who have the means to prepare for it, to hire tutors and buy prep books. My school is good about trying to mitigate this discrepancy by sponsoring practice tests required for all students and buying prep books for the school library, but the ACT still remains biased.

For me, college readiness consists of two main factors: academics and maturity. Academics is important—students need to have some foundational knowledge before going through rigorous college courses. However, maturity and responsibility are just as, if not more important. College is unique in that students must learn to self-regulate their schedules. Even the most intelligent students will fail in college if they don't learn to effectively manage their lives. However, I think my school defines college readiness in a more strict, academic sense, using only the ACT to determine if students are college ready.

We have many programs—from extra help after school to free ACT classes—to help students become academically ready. However, no one really teaches us how to be responsible, to manage our own finances or deposit a check. Personally, I feel academically prepared to attend college. I know I'm prepared in terms of maturity and responsibility—experiences like my parents' divorce when I was young have taught me to manage my own life when no one else could help me. But I still believe that these critical skills should be taught to all high school students.

High schoolers have tough lives, with constant academic and social stress. And students are often thought of as just numbers to report—ninety-nine percent are college ready, ninety-eight percent will attend college—but administrators need to remember that we are real people, who will soon be left to make it on our own. The transition from high school to college is stark and abrupt, and it's a change that sometimes forces unprepared students out of the education system.

It's time that our education considers not just academics, but also maturity, practical skills, and psychological wellness and readiness to take the leap to further education. Even in a school that thrives with numbers, I sometimes feel like the individual beneath all the statistics is sheltered and silenced. To the eye of the public, we are amazing. Why should we try to fix anything that doesn't seem to be broken in the way policy measures?

The Givens
Robert

"Both of my parents obtained master's degrees, and they expect me to do just the same."

I was recently elected as the president of my private Catholic school's culinary club by the other members. We get to cook whatever food we want every other Monday after school for no extra charge. This is made possible by the large student body of about thirteen hundred people. The students, or the parents of students, have to pay thousands of dollars to learn at this private school. This abundance of students leads to exorbitant amounts of money pumping in and out of the school. The funds available lead to yearly renovations like a new cafeteria or a million dollar indoor golf facility and over fifty clubs with thirty more sports programs. This allows for me to pursue my interests in volleyball, fishing, cooking, and newscasting.

The extra money and students also allow for many different classes and levels of classes such as honors and AP classes. These classes give me more of a challenge than others and would allow me to, potentially, earn college credit. Many times, I would sit doing homework past one in the morning wondering if the "college preparatory" part was really worth it. Was the preparation really worth the stress and the amount of sleepless nights I had experienced?

The excessive workload given by the teachers not only leads to students staying up late, but it harms the relationship between students and teachers. When asked their opinions about certain teachers, students respond, "Oh yeah, I hate him and his class." That could solely be because of the excessive workload and sleepless nights. Typically, teachers and students get along quite well. They joke around with each other and sometimes play little pranks with each other. This shows that they care. It shows the teachers care about the students and the students care about the teachers.

This year, a student fell asleep during class, probably because of a sleepless night before school. Instead of jugging him, the equivalent of sending a student to detention, the teacher walked over to his desk and tied the student's shoelaces to the desk in front of him. This was a classy prank which caused no harm to anybody. Laughs were shared with the whole class, even the kid who fell asleep. This teacher is one of the most well-liked employees of my school. He shows that he cares about the students, which leads to them respecting and caring for him. He even knows and relates to students on a first name basis.

This workload is also kind of expected though. Both of my parents obtained master's degrees, and they expect me to do just the same. There have even been pushes which imply I need a doctorate in some field. These expectations require that I do well and try my hardest, even in high school. Unfortunately, these are expectations and not realities. I plan on going to college for sure, but I do not do the best in school. I try, that is for sure, but I don't always reap the fruits of my labors.

For example, I definitely struggle in Spanish. I have had bad teachers in my past, which may impact my current grade in the class, but it also does not help that I have never spoken a lick of Spanish in my home. My parents do not know hardly more than a word in any language other than English, which harms me when it is time to study. I am fortunate that my parents care about me, want me to succeed, and will even help me study for big tests,. But it is not helpful that my parents cannot help me at all in Spanish, a class that kicks me and my GPA in the rear with every test.

Part of the reason for this struggle is the fact the teacher is somewhat difficult to work with. He wants me to succeed, I think, but he grades me harder than other students. I really do not know why, and I do not know what I ever did to him, but he continues to grade me harder than anybody else in my class. I recognized this and went to my counselor to solve the problem. I have a good relationship with my counselor. He goes to my church, and I really do not feel bad or ashamed going to him for help whether it is academic or just life advice. I went to him, and he helped me solve the problem.

Unfortunately, I will not have him as a counselor next year. Instead I will have a college readiness counselor. I guess he is there to make sure we, as students, are ready for college and know what to expect. He will help us apply to colleges in the beginning of the year by sending our transcripts and other important information. That is what college readiness is in my opinion. I believe it is just fulfilling all the required steps and knowing what to expect in college. It is basically just being prepared for college. I have prepared by taking AP classes to earn college credit and by taking the ACT. So far I have taken the ACT three times. I have a twenty-nine right now, which is a good score and is well above average, but it is not as good of a score as what I want. I want a thirty-two at least. This will put me in a good position to get into a lot of the colleges I would like to attend.

My ACT score has risen every time I have taken the test so far, but I still do not think it reflects how college ready I am. I am in the top five percent of my class, which is an exceptionally smart class, and yet I barely reach the top eight percent with my ACT scores. This may not be a huge gap, but it definitely makes a difference when applying to highly selective schools like Duke and the University of Miami in Ohio. It also makes a huge difference in scholarship money. Most schools give out some scholarships for achieving a thirty or over on the exam. A twenty-nine is so close, but it does not qualify. Because I have to pay for college mostly by myself, this scholarship money makes a difference. That is why I believe colleges should look at more than just the ACT. It is good that they look at GPA, both weighted and unweighted, because it shows class difficulty and how well the students do in those classes.

However, there are underlying factors that colleges will never be able to see or understand that should influence a college's decision of admitting students. Some students go through tragedies that affect their studies and others are not in a positive environment for learning. This harms their test scores which harms their chances of getting into a good college. Colleges will never see these underlying factors that seem to determine if somebody is "college ready." I don't really know how we should fix that though.

The Givens
Rainesford

"I genuinely thought I must have been the only one having a hard time—that's how absent conversation surrounding emotional readiness, emotional intelligence, and resilience is."

At varying points, I've been a student in Montessori school, public school, and even school online. That gave me a unique perspective on education and an enduring belief that learning is so much more about who we are and want to be as people than any grade or test score. Unfortunately, that foundation of believing education should be about the whole person went out the window as soon as it came time to apply for college. Leading up to my freshman year, I applied to an insane number of colleges without much awareness of what I was looking for, thinking that good grades in high school and a loose idea of what I wanted to major in would be enough to bridge my own college readiness gap. A sinking feeling in my stomach permeated every move I made toward college—even as I paid my deposit, unpacked boxes in my dorm room, and went through orientation, my decision felt rushed and just wrong. At the time, saying "I'm not ready" felt like the equivalent of "I'm not going at all."

Like most college freshmen, I was nervous about the "normal" parts of the transition, like living with a roommate for the first time. But I truly believed that as long as I continued to study hard, get good grades, and attempt to get involved on campus, everything would be fine. After all, most students see people go off to college every year seemingly without issue. College is presented as the culmination of over a decade of educational preparation, the next step that is considered a given. Unless you're struggling in classes with grades to demonstrate that, we very rarely consider other kinds of college readiness: emotional awareness, self-agency, ability to cope when things get rocky. I wasn't aware that any of those were crucial strengths. It seemed like a given that since my grades were good, I was prepared.

It became obvious within weeks of my first semester that while I may have been academically ready for college, personally, I was not equipped to navigate the transition at all. I looked around and saw other students having picked the perfect major, juggling the stress of college so effortlessly, and making friends with no problem. It felt like the opposite of my own experience, like I was staring inward with my nose pressed against the glass at something that seemed utterly out of reach. I went out of my way to get involved, just like we tell students to do. Feelings of isolation and failure seeped into everything I touched: I couldn't find a group of friends and was juggling a full course-load with a part-time job. The combination of being strung out over trying to be successful and feeling incredibly lonely left me so depressed I could hardly get out of bed.

In these situations, we hope students will reach out for help. Unfortunately, I mostly did the opposite: I became withdrawn, increasingly anxious, and, in a last-ditch attempt to control what felt like an out-of-control situation, stopped eating. I did reach out to one professor I had a good relationship with, explaining that something was wrong, that this wasn't working. He was puzzled by a student excelling academically who claimed she wasn't doing well, and encouraged me to stick it out.

What that conversation underscores to me in retrospect is how easily we fall into the trap of viewing students as just students, as though their academic identities are somehow separate from the rest of their personhood. In reality, students are complex human beings who have things happening personally, professionally, and at home that undoubtedly affect their work in the classroom. Most of the time, when I hear adults talk about students needing to be resilient or toughen up, it is to overcome a bad grade. We ignore the rest of the narrative: If we spend years of K-12 education telling students a bad grade could destroy their future, of course that bad grade will feel insurmountable to them. If we tell them there's something wrong if they can't make friends, of course they'll feel devastated when life on campus isn't clicking. It doesn't matter how academically astute we are if students feel like they're drowning in their own failure with no support or means of coping.

I genuinely thought I must have been the only one having a hard time—that's how absent conversation surrounding emotional readiness, emotional intelligence, and resilience is. We spend years getting students ready for the transition to college, but that effort seems to halt once orientation is over. College is four years of transition—of growing into who you will be. It says something that anxiety is the number-one diagnosis on campuses, and what that should tell us is we have to be more invested in what happens to students once they're there.

By the end of the year, I was so burnt out, exhausted, and frankly, sick, that I decided the best move was to jump off the wheel and take some time away from school, which felt like the opposite of resilience at the time. No one likes to feel like the person who can't handle something or can't stick it out. I needed to reconfigure my education and felt stepping away from the pressures of the university environment was the best means to do that.

That's when my definition of resilience completely, thankfully, shifted: It isn't just about getting through something. Sometimes, it means breaking down to rebuild and bouncing back.

Once out of school, I learned to persevere in a different way: I took on jobs and internships in fields related to my major, which helped me feel that I was moving my education forward in a different way. I met friends and mentors who I had more in common with than toga parties and reestablished my own ability to be confident in my decision-making. That self-agency—also called "phenomenal will"—is what put me back together. It allowed me to gain clarity over who I was and why I wanted to be in college to begin with. Mostly, it made me hopeful, which, turns out, goes hand-in-hand with resilience. Research shows hope is a bigger indicator of academic success than GPAs or SAT scores, and it proves that resilience doesn't just mean grit or blindly working hard. Hope is the belief that life has meaning, and that if you'll continue on, you'll find yours.

Out of school, that's exactly what happened to me. Had I not taken time to create self-agency, hope, and resilience, I wouldn't have returned to school and certainly wouldn't have graduated. I wouldn't have found friends, or gotten comfortable in my own skin. I definitely wouldn't be going to graduate school in the fall. It changed the entire course of my education, and by extension, my life.

Adam Grant, who wrote a book on resilience with Sheryl Sandberg, said in a recent commencement speech: "You need resilience to stay true to yourself on the days when others lose faith in you."

That second part—staying true to yourself—is self-agency. It is the most underestimated tool students need for college, and it is what gives us the capacity to not only be better students, but more compassionate, confident, capable people.

I was lucky to have supportive parents who were swift to lend a listening ear and take me seriously, even if their own experiences differed from mine. That support was crucial to sparking resilience, something we can't do alone. Studies show students who are invested in their communities and believe they can make meaningful contributions actually perform better academically. My own experience with resilience highlights the belief that we would be better served supporting students as individuals even outside academics. That combination of hope, resilience, and self-agency isn't just what will help students transition to college, but what will enable them to shape fulfilling, meaningful lives as well.

Part Three
The Dismissers

There are students who are not planning on going to college after high school.

It could be because they are heavily influenced by a surrounding culture in a community that doesn't view college as a viable choice. It could be that the financial burden of going to college is overwhelming. It could be that they feel oppressed by a school curriculum that doesn't allow them to explore their passions or that they simply don't feel prepared. Or it could be that there is an adult in their lives they look up to most who is not encouraging them.

Whatever the case may be, these are the students who dismiss the very premise of college as a path to a larger life.

They are the Dismissers.

It is interesting to note that some of the students in this part begin by explaining how much they would like to go to college but wind up talking themselves out of it by the end. Their ambivalence suggests that perhaps they are more open to conversations about college readiness than they would seem to be on the surface, a lesson perhaps that the Dismissers should not be so quickly dismissed.

The Dismissers

Charlie

"I'm smart. I know I am—just don't have time. And from what I have seen from my parents and how their lives turned out, I know college won't really be for me."

Um, right now

I'm kind of a tossup between a technical school and going into a career. With time, I've come to lean away from college. Both of my parents went to college. They both have their four-year degrees and did all the hard work, but just look at where it got them. They are still here in this county along with everyone else who didn't go to college. The only difference is that they had a lot more debt.

They are encouraging me to take dual credit classes, AP classes, honors. They want me to be mentally prepared for a more intense learning environment. Well, I mean, they're not great but, I mean, I understand why I need to take them. I haven't told my parents really that I'm not going to college, so for now, I just have to bear with the difficult classes.

The only way I could to go college anyway was if I got a scholarship, which if we are being honest here, is just not going to happen. Before, I was hoping to get a scholarship, based on my ACT score and my level of honors classes and stuff like that. But we have more important problems and better places to put our money than an education. There's a lot of people in our house; that means that there are a lot of mouths to feed. While my dad does have a degree, he's a school teacher, and school teachers don't make a lot of money. I think it is really ironic that a teacher's son isn't going to go to school anymore.

Back home, it is a full house. There's seven people in total: my two parents and five kids. On top of that, I have two more siblings that don't live with me. Just because it is a full house though doesn't mean it's big. We share bedrooms, sometimes three in a really small bedroom with one bed. I'm one of the oldest, so I have always learned to look out for the younger kids.

But, you know, you grow up around it, you get used to it. I don't really think much of it. Every once in awhile, I think to myself, *Man, it'd be great to be an only child, you know?* I come home everyday after school and there are four-year-olds screaming and demanding that I take care of them.

I am a lot older, so I "got to" take care of my siblings during their toddler years when my parents were working, especially in middle school. This meant no time for homework, studying, or even getting a job. No hanging out with friends, no late night movies, no fun, let alone any time to think twice about the formulas I learned in class. I wasn't really doing well in class anymore, and it was hard to keep up in high school. I'm smart. I know I am—just don't have time. And from what I have seen from my parents and how their lives turned out, I know college won't really be for me.

I mean, the ACT tells me the same thing. I wouldn't say it's a really good score, but last time I took it, I got a twenty-four. I made like a thirty-one and thirty in English and reading, but I made a seventeen and eighteen in math and science which really dropped my composite. Like, halved my composite. I didn't meet benchmarks in those classes, so if I go to college, I will have to take remedial courses.

I'm really good at English. It just makes sense to me. I remember in the fifth or sixth grade, I had to take a standardized test, and the results told me that I was already at a high school level. My mother got a degree in English, so you know, I grew up around books and literature. But then again, my dad's a math teacher, and you saw how that score ended up.

So basically, according to my test score, I'm not ready to go to college. I am not upset. It just validated what I already knew to be true. I think as far as the brain power goes, I could be ready. I could do well if I really wanted to, but I just don't anymore.

My friends didn't always think the same thing, but they do now. They don't even graduate high school 'cause, you know, their families are struggling, and they need to work on the farm. They might graduate high school, but that's as far as they get before they go to another huge factory around here.

At one factory, they make bread rolls, and at the other, they make like cups and plastic stuff. And y'know, that's like the backbone of this county. The cup factory has the highest employment rate of the people in this county, by like four times.

Most people here would like to go to college. They won't admit it to you, but they do. They aren't willing to work for it though. It would have to be handed to them on a silver plate. If someone said "Hey, you can go to college, drop everything and go to college. It's completely paid for. It's free. Go on ahead, do it," then I think would. But this is not a rich community. And college, it's expensive. And I think that what stops a lot of people from doing that, from going to college, is the cost.

Our counselors don't do much, to be honest. You didn't hear me say that. They're only in your classes, and that's about it. They can help you sign up for the ACT. They can help you get signed up for college class. We have dual credit or AP. That's about it. You know, as far as getting ready for college stuff like that, there is no one—except the GEAR UP counselors. They are the best. My parents have tried to help, but it's pointless. The playing field has changed a lot since their time in college.

There is a whole side of college that no one in school even acknowledges. It is all just focused on academics and not focused at all on—well, life in college. You know, the whole self-sufficiency part. I mean in my household, you have to be self-sufficient in a way, just because there's so many of us. Parents can't take care of everybody, especially as you get older. I do my own laundry. I cook dinner. But I don't think I'll be ready to be just dropped into a college campus right now. I don't know anything about the college environment. I just don't. We go to the campus visits and stuff, and we drive up there and stay for a couple hours. They show us all their fancy buildings and everything, but that just drives me away more than making me excited for college. It is scary, and I would rather not go at all.

My teachers disagree with the decision I have made. They think that I am ready, but I don't believe them at all. They are just saying those things because they have to. It has gotten to the point of where, these last few days, they have even tried to get me to go to technical school. I always thought that technical school was not something you did, really.

It's been basically shoved into our faces, "Go to college, go to college, go to college." I thought that's the only option you had. And now, as I'm opening other doors, seeing what else there is, I'm finding that you don't necessarily have to go to college. There's other options. It is just too bad that I found out about it so late. It just seems like a lot of work that I don't want to bother with. I can still end up as successful as my parents without school. No thank you.

The Dismissers
Connor

"A lot of people don't understand why I'm trying in school if I don't even want to go to college."

One thing I like about my high school is the teachers. The teachers are so nice. They're willing to work hard with you, they want to see you succeed, and they don't mind staying after school after hours, without pay, to help out a student who really needs it. That is the number one thing that stands out to me. Not the classes I'm offered, or the cafeteria food that I have to eat, or the dress codes that we have to follow.

One thing I don't like about my high school is the half of the so-called cool kids, because they feel like school is a waste of time. They always disrespect each other and their teachers, which makes me mad. Why do you feel the need to get on an adult? They're just trying to help you, and you are disrespecting them. We are all trying to learn, and you're distracting everyone else from learning. It doesn't make it cool.

The problem is continuous. It is odd for me to walk into a class and not have students argue or pick a fight with the teachers, and, what is worse, the teachers don't seem to know how to control it anymore. And I'm not the only one that sees this as a problem. Every single one of my friends, most of us enrolled in general classes, see the same thing.

What really gets on my nerves is there's a bunch of these girls, and they will talk and yell. The teacher could even be talking about a very important concept and they would still be screaming. They don't listen to the teacher as an authority figure, and that just makes the cycle worse. The teachers have no option but to be meaner, and the students lash out even more.

How does this entire loop even start? I don't even know. I think it all begins with a lack of communication and cooperation between the faculty and the student body. Students feel like their opinions don't matter, and they want to give teachers a taste of their own medicine. They want to somehow let the adults know how it feels to be silenced. I always feel like my classes have too many rules, too many strict guidelines, too many standards, too many hoops I have to jump through to get a good grade. I understand that being mean to my teachers is not the way to solve the issue, but I bet it feels good.

Most of the kids in my classes don't even want to go to college, which would explain why they don't care anymore about their grades. I don't want to either, but I still try my best. I'm a senior now, but next year I want to work in low-budget films because I eventually want to be an actor. Hopefully, I can make my way up there. I'm actually trying to start a YouTube fan film, but it's going to be a long wait. I have to get the money, I have to have a script.

Late at night, I will be like up thinking about it, listening to music. I'm so creative, I know I am. I will be listening to music and have scenes play in my head. Oh, this song will fit in this scene. This is how this scene should go! I tell my friends all about it, and they always say, "Let's just make it!" They are almost as enthusiastic as I am.

I just wish that there was a place in school where I could let my creativity run wild as much as when I'm listening to music at 2 a.m.

I tried to get involved in my theater group, but everything is already created. The scripts are decided by the teachers; the scenes are already planned out. Even the tech group that runs all the lights and music backstage is handed the soundtrack. We never do anything original, and when I tell my teachers, they always say that we don't have the time, or that it is too much work to start from scratch. They tell me that if I really wanted to get involved, I should audition for a role. But I know how many people come to see the production, and I knew I couldn't perform in front of that many people. They don't take me seriously. I am only a general student after all.

What's even worse though is that everyone loves the sports team more than the arts department. They get so much funding; everyone always goes out and cheers them on. They have events, games, their own cheerleaders, and sometimes, days off before their big games. I think the teachers feel like that too, that sports are everything. The arts are kind of pushed aside. With the plays, they don't really care. They make our show tickets cost a lot of money because that is our only revenue. But with sports, you can get into the game for free if you wear a certain shirt, a certain color. They can afford to do that.

My friends tease me all the time. They tell me that I have to audition anyways. They think I can't do it. Sometimes I believe them and wonder if I should give up on this dream I've created and think about something more realistic, like a manufacturing or factory job after I graduate.

The teachers try and fight with me about it. They don't understand why college isn't the right choice for me. I always tell them I don't want to go to college, and they ask why not. I tell them that I want to be an actor, and you don't have to go to college for that. You don't need to waste thousands of dollars to be eligible to work on low-budget films.

I mean, I was always on the edge about college. I guess I finally made my decision when I was in middle school around eighth grade. I was like, "If I ever go to college, I would want to go to one that's in town, less than an hour drive." But then when I actually got there, I just knew it wasn't for me. I visited their campus a couple times in the years afterwards, and I loved it. I've seen others across the state, but I liked this one university the best. I know a lot of people there, who graduated from my high school. I don't know, I just don't think it's for me.

I know a cool girl who goes there, and she takes acting classes. I tried sitting in with her on the courses and talked to her about it, and I just didn't like what they had to offer. This university was the only one I could see myself attending, and it was the only one I knew I could somewhat afford. But if I didn't like the classes in the major I wanted to get, I decided it wasn't worth it. It's not for me. I'm not even going to apply.

I haven't even taken the ACT yet this year. I was going to, but I couldn't because something happened with my picture, and now I have to wait until February to take it. I uploaded my profile photograph, and I didn't know that the system hadn't processed it or saved it before I logged out of my account. The teachers kind of waited until the last minute to fix it. They couldn't fix mine, and I couldn't take it this past Saturday. I felt really bummed out. I had studied a lot, and, this time around, I even took a course prep guide to help me raise my score. Some of my favorite teachers even took the time after school to work with me individually on my math and reading skills.

A lot of people don't understand why I'm trying in school if I don't even want to go to college. Why bother getting good grades or raising my ACT score? I think my example just goes to show that every student, regardless of if we make the decision to continue our education after high school, has the ability to be engaged and present. Just because we don't want to go to college doesn't automatically make us the "bad kids" or the "delinquents" like everyone labels us.

Right now, I'm just working hard trying to get my grades up. Trying to get my grades up so I can graduate. And after that, I will just work at the job I have now, making the money, and trying to find a local acting class, or school and just go from there.

My dad is totally up for it. He is the type of person that will motivate me, make me feel good. Just out of nowhere, I will be sitting there in the living room, watching a movie, and he will be like, "You could be that guy. You can be that guy on TV right there. You can be a superhero." Because that's what I want to play. I think everyone is like that. Everyone wants to leave their own legacy, to be remembered. Everyone wants to be that new song you can't stop listening to.

The Dismissers
Joseph

"I don't really want to go to college anymore."

If there is one thing I have to say about this school, it's that the teachers are biased. They're unfair. The school is against us, and no, that is not extreme. Not even a little.

We have "choices" in our classes. We are assigned classes, and we get to choose. And if they coincide, great. If they don't, oh well. So, you know, this year I signed up for a welding class, one accounting class, and two different business classes. That's all I signed up for. I got two welding classes and an agricultural science class—which I didn't sign up for.

It is a trend that I've caught onto in my classes at this school. Not just for me, but for a lot of my friends as well. Academic courses aren't as valued as career ones. I tried to take classes in subjects I'm interested in, like math and business, but I end up enrolled in more agriculture and welding. The school doesn't think that a lot of their kids are capable of anything more than high school. They don't think that their kids can go to college and do well there, so they try to prepare them for careers instead. They don't realize that some of us are actually interested in those fields. They don't want to believe that anyone can be different than the culture that they know.

If this were to happen my freshman or sophomore year, I would have been upset. I probably would have gone to the counselors and tried to get my schedule changed, but now, I decided that it is just not worth the hassle.

My sophomore year, I was forced to take Spanish II. I didn't want to, but they forced me.

I took Spanish I because it was required. Spanish II was optional, yet the principal forced me to take it. I had no choice. I said, "No, I don't want this class." "Well, you have to have it." "No, this is an optional class. I do not want this class." "You have no choice. You have to take this class." It was the principal. There's not much I could do. I confirmed later that it was optional. I got over it. I was used to having the adults not know anything about the schooling system. I don't really want to go to college anymore. I take business and math classes because I find them interesting, and that's it. When enough people treat you a certain way, you begin to believe it.

Another way the school is against us is the teachers. They don't really care about us, for the most part. There are a few who do. But my math teacher does not care if we succeed. She just cares if we make good grades and make her look good. And she's very biased. Just the other week, I was late to class by a few seconds, and so were four other people right behind me. But I was the only one who got a tardy.

Along with that, they don't give us information for the FAFSA. I've heard about it many, many times, but I have no clue what it is. I've heard it about eighteen times today. It's something about federal aid? I don't know what it is. I mean, I've heard that you can get scholarships elsewhere, like military family scholarships. A large part of my family is in the military: grandfathers, uncles, cousins. Thankfully, not my father. He tried, but he didn't get in.

I wanted to go to college to be an accountant, because I love math. I love controlled chaos, where it's challenging enough that you have to work at it, but you don't lose control. Controlled chaos is my favorite thing. I've looked at scholarships, like the military scholarships, and I'll have to go get a blood test to see if I'll get a scholarship for foreign blood. My family's told me that I'm part American Indian, like Cherokee. So, I'm going to try to get scholarships for that.

I am not taking any college or dual credit classes, but I have taken all of the business classes that I can. I've taken Basic Computer Apps, Advanced Computer Apps, Accounting I and II, and Economics. I've gotten Microsoft Office certified too.

I've taken all the steps. I did what they told me to do. I found what I like and followed through with "in-depth" study. But now that it is time to go to college, I don't think that I can.

I hear about "college readiness" all the time. It's usually paired with "college and career ready," and I don't know exactly what it is. I can tell from the name that it's supposed to get me college ready, but I don't know how or what I need to do to be college ready.

Someone asked me if I had seen a counselor, and I responded, "We have counselors?" I don't think I've ever seen the school counselor, but I talk to my GEAR UP counselor a lot. I've heard of the mythical legends of school counselors, but I've never actually spoken to one.

To be honest, I have no idea where the benchmarks for the ACT are set, but I bet I am college ready at least for math. Even if I did meet benchmarks for all subjects, I don't feel ready. I've seen colleges and how they work. You know, very large classrooms, one professor. I don't like it. A test score does not make you college ready. I could be fine socially though. I can't cook anything fancy, but I can do my own laundry. I could survive.

But I'm not going to go to college because of the cost. As far as financial preparation, well, I have a job at the mall. And, you know, it's stereotypical. I work at McDonald's.

A lot of my friends and people I know don't want to go to college. Just like me. That's what it's like around here. One of my best friends doesn't think he'll go to college either. I think he'll become a hands-on type of person, mechanic or something. Another one of my friends wants to become a professional football player, so I guess he could go to college, but he wouldn't be going for the education. It's normal not to go to college here. It's the culture.

The "County Diet" is kind of the stereotypical culture here. It got its name from its prevelance in this county. The County Diet is meth and soda. It's called a diet partially because that is all we eat and because it makes you awfully skinny. Drugs are "in" here. You hear guys talking about dip and smoking marijuana or weed. You hear all of that kind of stuff. There are guys that say they drank so much over the weekend that they can't remember the weekend. That's our county. So, no, college is not our first priority. Stereotypically, this school is not a college type of thing. Guess I am just another one of those students.

My mom did not go to college because her family was not very wealthy, so she couldn't afford it. I don't know if my dad did. I never asked. He went to vocational school, but I don't know if he went to college. My grandmother didn't. The way college works for the people that do end up going is pretty similar. Usually the first time you go, you drop out, and it usually takes another try. I don't want that to be me.

Kids probably drop out because it's a lot harder than you would expect. You think it's going to be like high school where you just BS every paper and you'll be fine. No. I've heard the horror stories, and I am not going.

It's fine. Could be worse.

The Dismissers
Lilian

"Let's be realistic here. Why doesn't anybody in the school understand that I don't—can't—go to college?"

Most of the counselors and staff want us to go to college. Some of them couldn't care less; like, they don't put forth any effort. Some of them care way too much. It just depends on who you are talking to. But I've made my choice. I don't want to go to college. It's decided.

I just, I don't know. I feel like it's not for me. I struggle with high school really bad. It's just not been a great experience here for me.

Freshman year, I didn't come for the first two weeks. I got sick, and we didn't know what was wrong. I was in and out through freshman year. I had to start wearing a mask, doctor's orders. I was getting sick so often they thought that a mask would help support my immune system or something like that.

So then, I got treated differently from other people. A lot of kids were mean, rude, and not very nice. I had a lot of friends going into freshman year, but I was always in and out, so I lost them all. I was always behind. I barely managed to pass freshman year, like barely made it. My parents had to talk with the school and make sure that they weren't going to hold me back.

Sophomore year, I only went six weeks. I was home most of the time, and then, I didn't go back until the last three months of junior year.

I have a rare blood disorder. I had to be treated once a week, every week, and it still wasn't working. I was very sick. I got three blood clots in my liver, and my liver started shutting down. I barely even made it through that.

I didn't have any friends, you know. I guess people didn't really know just what to say. Then my family was sucked into it too. They were always worried and were always working to pay the medical bills. I had no one, basically.

I still have to go to the doctor a lot now. I'm still having problems, even now, a year and a half out. But the blood disorders are getter better. Right now, I am just struggling with the side effects of chemo. I am starting to experience short-term memory loss. I've had that ever since I got sick.

For example, if we learn something in class, I can remember it as long as we are talking about it. I'll know it perfectly then, but after a week, I'll forget it. Sometimes, I tell the people at school the same story multiple times, but they wait until the end to tell me that they have already heard it five times. They tell me that every time I tell it with the same excitement, as if I hadn't even told anyone about it before. They don't want to stop me since I'm so eager to share.

I get fatigued, like really, really tired. I can sleep twenty hours and barely function. It's just like, a lot. So that's why I was out sophomore year. When I came back junior year, I took a lot of credit recovery courses. I had to stay in one room for the entire day for three months. Now I'm actually in classes. Well, I was supposed to be. I had to go back to credit recovery because I stopped coming to school. This time, it was a transplant. I'm going to have to take that week by week and see what all's going to happen and how we're going to handle it.

I can feel it hurting me academically. It's really clear on the ACT. The dreaded ACT. See, that's another thing I can't stand. They stress me out because I can't remember stuff. To someone who has never been in my shoes before, this sounds like an awful excuse, but it really is the truth. I forget people's names and to lock my house after I leave, so why not a formula? And see, like the stuff they teach in class is totally different, so I don't remember it, and I don't meet my benchmark. The section I do very well on is reading because it requires no past knowledge, really, but it is still very difficult. My teacher helped me with that section one time. She made me read all of the passage and summarize it afterwards. I couldn't do it. Like, I would totally forget half the story as I read it. In the end, I didn't meet benchmarks.

In the years that I couldn't come to school, we tried homebound education. It was a great plan to continue my classes at home when I wasn't able to go to school due to my health. Teachers came to my house to catch me up on my classes, and at first it was a wonderful idea. I was very excited. But the teacher didn't know what she was doing, really. We got off schedule, and she didn't know the material. I fell behind again, and she didn't encourage me. She had the nerve to tell me, "Well, you're gonna fail. You're not gonna pass. Don't be surprised." So I just didn't do it. Half the teachers here at school don't motivate you. I don't think very many people realize it, but having someone to push you makes a huge difference.

We found another homebound teacher in the next few days. He'd come like twice a week, sometimes three times a week if we got a little behind. But he pushed me to do it, and I looked forward to our meetings because he didn't tell me I would fail.

So, I guess I'm not "college ready," whatever that means. They shove that phrase down your throat here, but they don't tell you what it is. I just don't understand why we have to do it 'cause half these kids don't even go to college. Like half this town, they don't go to college.

I have two fathers: my stepdad and my real dad. Neither of them went to college. My real dad works in roofing, and my stepdad works in a factory. My mom went to college, but she still works in a factory. I think she wants me to go to college to be successful and to be better than her. I think that's every parent's dream for their kid, but my parents, they want me to do what makes me happy.

But other kids are living paycheck to paycheck here. The pay is just not good. Kids don't even get to go to college. They have to live around here and get a job as soon as possible. And, for me, I don't think I live like that, I guess. I have everything I want and need, but some kids don't.

I just know college isn't for me, and people can't seem to understand that here. I need to work to help pay for these medical bills. That, and I don't think I would be able to do well socially. I get really nervous around people, to the point where I have to puke. Being in a classroom, it just makes me so uncomfortable. I didn't used to, but now I can't stand it. I struggle with all the work, and I have to stay after school three times a week just to even pass my math class. I've had to stay for other classes too. And I can't handle a lot of work. My body literally cannot take it. College is just not going to happen for me.

Here, everyone knows me. They know my name; they know my history. Like, if something happens to me, they know what to do. When you go to college, the professors don't really care. You're a grown adult. You're in college. You gotta be independent. I think I could count on somebody to at least give me help here, but in college, I just don't think it will happen.

Let's be realistic here. Look at where I come from. Look at all the money we owe. Look at my health. Look at the job I have to have. Do I really need to explain myself anymore? Why doesn't anybody in the school understand that I don't—can't—go to college?

Everyone thinks that this school is so great, but really it sucks, like big time. I had to fight so hard to get a high school education with this health. The principal is just cocky and uninformed about the school's issues. None of the staff is on the same page. I would go into school board meetings, and for a half hour before the meeting actually started, the staff would have to fill in the principal on all the issues we were going to talk about. Every time my mother and I attend these meetings to work with my circumstance, everyone is so rude. But mom, being the way she is, just kept on talking. So I literally had to fight, like tooth and nail, to get anyone in the school to help me. I just—I don't think it's a good place. And people move here thinking, "Oh, it's a good school." But it's really not. Not at all.

I mean, at least now I can tell someone about it, someone who will listen without having me fight for it.

The Dismissers
Claire

"I don't want to go study something that I don't like, and no one else seems to support what I want to do with my life. Recently, I've been thinking about just staying put."

You can tell whenever my teacher has a favorite 'cause he'll let them do anything they want and yell at the other kids. I've tried my hardest to make trouble in his class, but he just won't do anything. I'll listen to music. I'll be on my laptop. I'll do everything to try and get him mad at me, but he'll still give me A's. He just don't care. And all the other kids get yelled at and sent out of class.

In his class, sometimes you have to fight for a grade. Only sometimes does he let you whine or beg to bump up your letter grade, but most times there is nothing really you can do. You either do the work or you don't. He never makes you turn in an assignment, and most times, the students that talk to him before or after class and show the smallest bit of attention automatically get A's. We took a test the other day, and even though my peer and I missed the same questions, I got the higher grade.

After high school, I want to go to Morehead State University for four to six years, and then I want to go down to the medical school in Atlanta. I want to be a midwife. My mom says it's a risky choice, but I've had that plan since I was in the fifth grade, and I wanna stick with it. But my grandmother's trying to persuade me to another way. So are most of my teachers. My friends are just like, "So you're gonna leave us? Just like that?" Like, we're gonna leave each other sometime. I want to go to college, but I'm not sure anymore. Everyone else seems to be telling me differently. I don't want to go study something that I don't like, and no one else seems to support what I want to do with my life. Recently, I've been thinking about just staying put.

I had an art teacher last year. I told her what I wanted to do, and she just laughed. She laughed and told me, "You shouldn't even try. You don't have what it takes to do all of that hard work, and even if you did, you're going to work and end up wasting a lot of money. And you won't even finish the job." She wasn't really a nice person. She lost her job, but she had a point.

Everyone here is freaking out about the ACT. I just see it as a huge waste of time. I think it's only to show the school what you wanna do, like, how smart you are. But that's really it, there's no college readiness or anything. It's either you know it or you don't. Last year I met all of my benchmarks, but this year I'm pretty sure I didn't. I think it is funny how everyone else improved as I went down. Last year, I had a reading development class, and I've always had classes like that, but all of a sudden, they just throw me out. And I was like, "Oh dear, I won't have any help with this at all." I didn't really want to read anymore anyway. It was a hard class.

I don't know what college readiness is. I don't know what it stands for. I don't even hear anyone using that phrase. The only person that sometimes uses it is my GEAR UP counselor. What did you say the standards were? Meet benchmarks? Is that really it? Is that all we have to do is meet the benchmarks, and we're college ready? I still think it's useless. So according to that test, I was ready last year, but not anymore! See, even the test is telling me not to go to college.

I wanted to go before. I actually took college classes during the summer and stuff like that. I cried my first week. I wanted to go home.

Even if I wanted to go, I'm not sure what I'd do financially. I think if I do like FAFSA or stuff like that, I might be able to do it. I'm saving up right now. I have a few thousand dollars saved up, and I think that should be enough. I plan on not having any loans, but that's probably not going to happen. I haven't even thought about how I'm going to pay off my loans. All I know about loans is that I have to pay it back, that's all. If you threw me in college right now I wouldn't survive.

Now I'm thinking that most of my friends were right. It's probably a waste of time, waste of money. I probably shouldn't care anymore. I'm never going to go anywhere. That's how most people feel, and now I do too. I know most people, they haven't left this county because even their parents are from here, and they were taught they were never going to get anywhere. Like even my dad is from here. He never got anywhere. I wanted to get out of here, but it seems too hard.

Most of my algebra class thinks things like, "I'm going to drop out and get a job at the factory." Most of the guys in there, they're like, "I just don't see the point in here." They were all trying to get into the special needs class just so they could get an easy A. And they say around like their senior year, they're just gonna leave. They're not even going to get their degree or anything. They're just gonna go work. And everyone's just like, "Well good luck with that. Have fun." For the most part, the teachers don't care. I've heard some of them say, "We're here for a paycheck. That's it."

I think teachers should at least care about students. When I was younger, in like elementary school, somebody was bullying me, and I told one of my teachers, "I'm being bullied." The teacher immediately went up to the student, grabbed them by their collar, and dragged them to the office. I was just like, "Alright then." They didn't need to ask any questions or anything. I didn't even say names. They knew it was them. They treat us like adults when we need help, and they treat us like kids in the classroom when we need to be viewed as adults.

I don't want to talk about this anymore. Are we done?

Part Four
The Moonlighters

Not all high school students are full-timers.

Some students feel that they do not have the luxury to place their studies over everything else.

For thirty-five hours a week, these students are in school, listening to teachers talk about quadratic equations or the different branches of government.

But for the other 133, they are working long hours, taking care of their families, dealing with emotional trauma, or living paycheck to paycheck.

The discrepancy between these students' double lives can feel overwhelming.

They are the Moonlighters.

The Moonlighters have a fierce desire to get to and through college to improve their lives but typically have to shoulder the burden of many responsibilities beyond academics.

The Moonlighters are the ones who demonstrate superior resourcefulness and resilience but also the ones whose greatest strengths may not show up in their GPA and ACT scores.

The Moonlighters often carry the weight of the world on their shoulders with little to no recognition. Instead, they are successful in ways that most schools do not measure.

The Moonlighters
Brianna, Cate, Dalia, Kadisha, Madison & Natasha

"I'm the head of my household. I'm the dad of my family. I can't worry about myself because I know I've got my stuff together, but I worry about everyone else because I take care of everyone else."

We began this roundtable discussion with six girls in an urban high school as lightly as we could, starting with a question about what Jell-O flavored animal they would be. From the first moments of our encounter, it was clear this group was special. They were by far the loudest group in the room, and their bubbly personalities were infectious. At first, it appeared that this would be a breezy conversation, but when we started asking them about their plans for high school and beyond, the conversation went about as deep as it could go as fast as it could go. These students had so much to say.

. . .

Student Voice Team: I'd like you to go around and say your name, maybe an extracurricular activity you do or any clubs you are involved in, and then I want to know: If you could be a Jell-O animal, what flavor and animal would you be?

Brianna: Hi, I'm Brianna, and I do Pep Club right now. If I could be a Jell-O animal, I would be an orange flavored buffalo.

Kadisha: I'm Kadisha, and I would probably be a cherry cat.

SVT: Are you in any clubs or extracurricular activities?

Kadisha: I read, and I work.

Cate: I'm Cate, and I'm a part of Future Business Leaders of America.

SVT: Oh cool. That's awesome. What Jell-O animal would you be?

Cate: I'd be a cherry dolphin.

Dalia: My name is Dalia. I'm kind of boring.

Cate: She's a part of FBLA.

Dalia: Yeah, and I have two jobs. And I would be a blue raspberry horse.

Madison: My name is Madison. I am not a part of any clubs, but I work six days a week at a fast food chain here in town. If I could be a Jell-O animal, I would definitely be a grape llama.

Natasha: My name is Natasha. I'm not in any clubs right now, but I work at a daycare. I love kids. I'd be a blue raspberry starfish.

SVT: Okay, let's talk a little bit about where you live. How long have you guys lived here?

Brianna: On and off.

Cate: I've lived here since I was nine.

Dalia: Since like sixth grade.

Natasha: On and off since I was little.

SVT: So none of you guys were born here?

Brianna: Yeah I wasn't born here. I came here in like second grade and on and off since.

SVT: That's interesting. Let's get real now. Tell me about your high school. What do you like about it?

Cate: I think our school is really helpful because we're in a high poverty area. They do everything they can for the children there.

Brianna: The thing I like about it are the classrooms. I'm easily distracted, and I need a lot of extra help. Our classrooms are so small that we get personal time with our teachers, and a lot of the teachers take the initiative to stay after school and come help us.

Natasha: They're really involved.

Brianna: I love our teachers.

Dalia: I like the fact that our resources are endless too. You can go to our counselors, and they know people who can help too.

Kadisha: I like that they try to help you fill out your FAFSA and financial aid stuff.

Brianna: You have to take that extra step though. Because here, a lot of kids don't care, so the administration, not teachers, don't want to waste their time. They want you to come find them. But once you find them, they'll never let you go. Also, our principals and administrators are good too. For me personally, if I have problem, they fix it immediately.

Cate: But if it's "drama" problems, they aren't going to jump to fix it. You're supposed to be grown enough to deal with it. But if you're getting bullied or something, they'll help you out.

Natasha: The assistant principal will really do anything in his power to help.

Brianna: Yeah, definitely.

SVT: So it seems that you guys all have a pretty good relationship with your teachers, administrators, and principals. If someone has a problem, it seems that all of you have at least one person you can reach out to.

All of the girls nod their heads in agreement.

SVT: As of right now, what are your plans for college?

Brianna: Okay, well, the plan is to go to the University of Louisville (U of L) in the fall. I applied for a scholarship, so I'm really hoping to get that. But I'm using my FAFSA money to pay for most of it. I'm going to study business management and political science while I'm there. And maybe, I'll even throw for their track and field team.

Kadisha: I was going to start at the community college here because I don't know what I want to do yet. My FAFSA covers most of it. And then eventually, when I figure out what I want to do, I'll transfer to a university.

Cate: I don't know where I'm going yet. I've been accepted to a lot of places but I'm waiting on scholarships. Definitely staying in Kentucky though. I really want to study pre-vet, but I don't know.

Dalia: I want to go to Tuskegee University, in Alabama, for business marketing. But if I can't pay for it, I'll go somewhere here.

Natasha: I think I'm just going to go to the local university to study early childhood education. I love kids. I can't wait to teach.

Madison: Since I've already been going to community college. I'll just finish up my associates degree there and transfer to the local university.

SVT: Okay, your dream job for you would be?

Natasha: A preschool teacher probably, maybe kindergarten.

Dalia: I want to be an entrepreneur.

Cate: Right now, I would love to be a vet.

Madison: I want to be a pediatric nurse practitioner.

Kadisha: I honestly have no idea.

Brianna: I want to be president of the United States.

SVT: What!? Me too! I'll fight you for it.

Brianna: I'm serious, girl. I want it.

SVT: Okay fine, I'll just be your Vice President. I will gladly work under you. Okay, next question. Do you guys take any honors or AP classes?

Brianna: Not anymore.

Kadisha: We don't have any.

Cate: We had some last year, but not this year.

Dalia: I take college classes at the community college. You can take all your general education classes there, so this year I took Writing, Psychology, and like College Success or something like that. And then next semester, I'm taking Writing II and College Algebra.

SVT: Dude, that's incredible! That's so cool. We definitely don't have that at my school. Would any of you guys consider yourselves "honors kids" who take all honors classes?

Brianna: We were all honors kids together. When I first came into high school, they didn't know where to put me. They didn't put me in honors classes. Even when I was making and requesting my schedule, I would place myself in difficult honors classes, but they'd still put me in regular classes again. I didn't go to middle school here, so they didn't trust me.

SVT: Did you notice a difference in environment or teaching between the regular and honors classes?

Brianna: Oh yeah. Teachers in regular classes dumb everything down. I've always thought our school babies us and really dumbs things down. You can definitely see the difference in classes.

SVT: So with that, in the hallways and in the classrooms, can you see these divides that we're talking about?

Natasha: Not always. We sit with whoever we want at lunch and stuff, but when you walk into an honors class, you know it's an honors class by the kids in that class.

Dalia: But people in our school automatically assume that if you're in regular classes you don't care and you don't want to be there.

SVT: Do you think, at your high school at least, these kids who are in only regular classes have the exact same opportunities as you guys as honors kids?

Brianna: They have the same opportunities as us, but our administration won't tell them that.

SVT: That's interesting. So I feel like I have a good understanding of who you guys are, what your school is like, and what you're interested in. Let's get into the good stuff now: the ACT.

Brianna: Don't even mention that test. I think it's a terrible way to test people! I hate it!

SVT: So I don't want to know your score, but tell me if you've taken the ACT. Raise your hand if you've taken it at least once?

All of the girls raise their hands.

SVT: So who is happy with their current score?

None of the girls are happy with their current score.

SVT: Have you all reached benchmark?

Brianna: Not in reading.

Natasha: I haven't in math.

SVT: Are you taking remediation classes or something to help your score go up?

Both Brianna and Natasha are taking remediation classes.

SVT: You guys have kind of already answered this, but to what extent do you think the ACT predicts how you'll do in college? Like one to ten what would you say?

Brianna: Four

Kadisha: I'd say like a five or a six. My score is fine, but I'm lazy and I hate classwork. That's really bad for college and my score doesn't show that.

Cate: I'd say probably a six.

Dalia: I'm neutral so a five, I guess.

Madison: I'm a five or six. Just because I've been taking college classes and I feel ready.

Natasha: I'm a four.

Brianna: I have terrible test anxiety, so I think it's unfair for them to only use that score when I'm nervous.

SVT: Okay, so let's talk a little bit about the financial stuff. You don't have to answer this if you don't want to but—

Dalia: —We're all poor. We can all agree on that.

All the girls agree and laugh.

Natasha: Our whole school gets free lunch.

Cate: Our whole school gets it, but even if we didn't, most of us would qualify for free lunch.

SVT: So in terms of financial aid for college, do you know how you're going to pay for college?

Madison: All scholarship. There's no way I could pay without it.

Cate: A lot of us are trying for scholarships.

Madison: I have a plan because I'm poor, and I know that if I don't make a plan now, I'll just not do it. You just have to push yourself, man.

Dalia: Yeah, we are all poor.

Madison: My parents just don't want to help.

SVT: Wow, you guys are so open about this.

Brianna: Yeah, my family lives from paycheck to paycheck, and we're just broke, broke, broke.

Madison: We understand how life really is.

SVT: So let's talk about family. Who do you live with?

Brianna: My mom.

SVT: Does she work?

Brianna: Yes. She's a manager at McDonald's.

Kadisha: I live with my mom and she's on disability. But I have a job at Panera.

Brianna: Do we all have jobs here?

All the other girls have jobs.

Brianna: Okay cool. Just checking. I thought most of us here worked, but I wanted to make sure. I pay bills and work at Arby's.

SVT: Pay bills? What does that mean?

Brianna: Like, pay bills—actual bills. Not just a phone bill! Like, water and stuff.

Cate: I live with my dad, and he's a construction worker.

SVT: Do you have any siblings?

Cate: Three brothers, and I work at Frisch's.

Brianna: Two real siblings, and my mom's pregnant with another one.

Kadisha: Three sisters and five brothers.

Dalia: I live with my mom, and she's a LPN (Licensed Practical Nurse). I have a lot of siblings. I always forget how many I have. I think I have seven. I live with four of them. I work at the animal shelter.

Madison: I have two little sisters, and they both live with me, my mom and dad. But my dad has a job sometimes. He likes to stop going to his job and wait the ninety days out and get his job back. He works at a factory. My mom works at Kroger, and she makes way more than my dad. And I work at Bob Evans. My sisters are thirteen and nine.

Natasha: Well, I live with my cousin Jane. She has four kids and she's a single mom, so I'm the only one in the house with a car and a job. And I work at a daycare.

SVT: What are your family's attitudes about college?

Madison: My mom doesn't care.

Brianna: My mom really wants me to go.

Natasha: My dad is proud of me and wants me to go, but they aren't really supporting me.

SVT: Do you see college as something that is necessary?

All of the girls enthusiastically agree.

Dalia: Especially nowadays. If you want a good job, you have to have a college degree.

Brianna: Power is in education. If I go to talk to someone or debate about something, the more I know and more facts I have, the more I walk away winning.

SVT: What are your fears about college?

Kadisha: I'm scared of failing.

Brianna: The only thing I'm scared of is something tragic happening at home while I'm away. Everyone at my home is getting sick, and it makes me scared. I'm a strong person, but I worry over my mom. If something happened to her while I'm in college, I know that would mean me dropping out. If my mom needs me, I'm leaving.

Madison: I'm so scared of my dad dying.

Natasha: Me too! I feel like I'm eighteen, and I shouldn't have to worry about my dad dying, but I do. And it's not even like it's health stuff. It's his fault.

SVT: So what exactly are you worried about?

Madison: Well my dad, he likes drugs. He loves it. He likes to "try" heroin every few months, and he's overdosed a couple of times. I'm terrified of getting that phone call like, "Hey your dad's dead," and I'll have to drop out of school.

Brianna: I'm the head of my household. I'm the dad of my family. I can't worry about myself because I know I've got my stuff together, but I worry about everyone else because I take care of everyone else. My mom gets depressed easily, so when I say I'm the head of the household, I'm head of the freaking household. My mom's not mentally strong.

Madison: Same! I have to wake my sisters up for school, brush their hair, and everything. I'm my parents' therapist. I am the one making sure they get out of bed and go to work. Whenever they're going through something, they talk to me. They can't talk to each other because they hate each other.

Dalia: Of course if my mom asks me for fifty dollars, I'm not going to tell her no because we won't have water, and that's normal. But like, I think I'm "gucci."* My mom's dependable and supportive. I'm grateful. But I feel like every teenager here helps their parents. It's just common sense to me. It's just nature.

Brianna: See, my mom had me so young that she decided I was her friend. I've helped raise my brothers and sisters. I even helped raise some of my older cousins. I remember when I was younger, in my grandma's house, I was like four or five, warming up dinner for these seven-year-olds and making sure everyone took their bath, brush their teeth, and was in bed. My grandma decided I was going to take care of everyone. So it's natural for me to want to help, but I've never really been a kid.

Madison: Yeah, I'm a mom. My thirteen-year-old sister was born, like, ten days after I turned four, and my dad was really bad on drugs then. Crack was really big back then, and my mom worked at Wendy's full time and I was babysitting. I wasn't allowed to hang out with friends after school because I had to go home and take care of my two little sisters. And I hated it. But then I realized that they have to work. I had to learn how to cook chicken noodle soup when I was four!

SVT: It's amazing to hear your stories. You all perservere through everything life throws at you. You're strong and powerful.

Natasha: Sometimes I really feel like a failure though.

Brianna: But I'm proud to know that if something happened right now, I could support myself.

Natasha: I have no one to motivate me. I motivate them, but no one's helping me or motivating me, nobody.

Kadisha: I think I would rather be sheltered than go through what I've been through. Because like, I don't even want to go into it because it will probably make me cry. But it's just been a lot of emotional stuff. I've been in foster care and been molested, and I would rather none of that happen.

Madison: I had my grandpa's best friend molest me, so I understand.

What were we talking about again?

Kadisha: School.

Madison: Oh yeah… school.

The Moonlighters
Mackenzie

"I work because I have to, not because I want to. I work because if I don't, I know that my house will have no water and no electricity. So, I'm sorry if I sometimes don't have my homework. I'm trying my best here."

So I'm a senior in high school, and I'm going to graduate this year with, drum roll please, about a third of the way to my associate degree! After this, I'll go and finish out at the local community and technical college where I took a lot of free college classes in my junior and senior years. They didn't really have enough classes for me at my high school, so I find myself off campus more than I find myself with the rest of the high school students.

I transferred to this area during my sophomore year. I was pretty ahead of the game when I got here compared to everyone else. I started getting high school credits in eighth grade, so by the time I got to this school, there wasn't much for me to do. I had electives, but that's about it. I had to drop out of a lot of AP classes I was taking back home because my current high school didn't provide them. They don't offer a lot around here, now that I think about it. But I mean, it's not like the lack of opportunities are actually mourned by anyone here. A lot of people at my school simply don't have any desire to take APs. However, for those of us who want to get more for college out of high school, AP classes would have been a huge benefit. If it wasn't for the local community college, I have no idea what I would do. I would probably feel suffocated, and I know that I wouldn't have the thirty-two credit hours I do now.

The school where I transferred from is a huge school. It's considered to be a really bad school by a lot of people, mostly because it's a very poor area and mostly African-American. I didn't want to transfer here at all, but I had to move. It's not all terrible, though. I like that I get to co-op, to leave early to go to work, and make some more money. But one problem here is that there's nobody to talk to if you have questions about your future or anything like that. There's one teacher who's helpful and there's the youth service lady, but those two are the only ones in the whole school who really care about where we're going and what we're doing after high school. Not many of the school staff are actually actively trying to help us.

For example, the ACT. I'm on campus for only an hour and a half each day, so I miss a lot of the meetings and announcements the other seniors get. A lot of the people who leave campus are in the same boat as me, but I'm more determined than others to keep up with what the school is doing when I'm not around.

I wasn't even aware we were taking the ACT until about a month before. The woman who told me about it said something about how I should have known. She told me that I should have signed myself up for it months ago. She didn't help me at all. And worst of all, she wasn't even my school counselor. I learned that I had to take the ACT from a professor at my community college. She was confused when she saw the students from my school come into classes in February and early March without any ACT textbooks. She was hesitant to ask us about it, especially when none of us seemed to be talking about this "extremely important" test in the first place. She was shocked when we didn't even know the state-mandated March test was coming up or that it was a requirement to graduate.

I ended up having a different teacher sign me up for it, and I did pretty well. I got a twenty-three, which was a lot better than a lot of my friends, including those that were taking college classes off campus with me. Apparently, the school helps students and encourages everyone to take the ACT multiple times, so it doesn't make any sense why they forgot to tell an entire group of students to take their first test. I just can't get over the fact that all the students who go off campus were forgotten about.

I filled out the FAFSA in October. I got out of class and met up with the guidance counselor. I had no idea how to fill it out, how to transfer grades to colleges, or anything like that. She did help me with that. However, I don't think there's much help for someone who's less active in seeking out what they need. I'm in the office all the time asking for different people to make sure I can get all this under control. Help is not just going to come find you here, so if you're not as assertive as me, you might be out of luck.

I have to be in charge of my own future. And almost everyone here doesn't care about their future. It's not that they don't want to go to college, it's more that they've accepted that they're poor and think they can't do it. They drop out because everyone else is doing it, and then they blame it on their financial situation.

But I am poor. I work because I have to, not because I want to. I work because if I don't, I know that my house will have no water and no electricity. Some people in my class pretend like they have it rough. They whine about having gross free and reduced lunch food, and they complain about being on a budget. If only they knew how hard it can actually get! If only they knew what it was like to work the scary night shifts at a fast food restaurant when the faces that come in aren't very friendly. If only they—and not just the students, but the teachers, the counselors, the administration—knew how some of us at this school go straight to work after school and don't go home before coming back to class the next day. So, I'm sorry if I sometimes don't have my homework. I'm trying my best here. At least I don't accept my fate like everyone else in this school. At least I'm trying to make something of myself.

It doesn't help how some teachers just say, "Well, you failed," when you do badly on a test instead of trying to help you get back up. Most classes don't have corrections. Once you fail, there's nothing you can do about it, and no one is willing to do anything for you. I feel like this way of thinking that the students here have, the hopelessness and resignation, is because of everyone.

The students feel like there's no one on their team. Their teachers don't support them, their parents don't support them, the administrators and counselors don't support them. Then they just decide to get a job wherever they can get one, either after graduating or after dropping out. A lot of people drop out to work just because they need the money now, and they don't see a realistic way they can get more education and a better career.

My best friend dropped out last year because her parents weren't trying to help her with anything, and she was trying to find information on financial aid. She wanted to figure out what she was going to do for college, but she ended up going to work at

McDonald's. I tried to talk her out of it, but she knew that she wouldn't be able to further her education after high school anyway, for financial reasons alone.

Her mom was furious. Her daughter was supposed to be the smart girl that saved the family from poverty. She told my friend that she was going to kick her out and a bunch of other stuff. She told her that she couldn't afford to feed her and have her under her roof. Now she lives with her boyfriend. That's not what you're supposed to be doing when you're eighteen years old.

But that was it; we don't even talk anymore. If someone had just helped her get financial aid, if someone in the school just pushed her and told her she should stay, she might have had a chance to go to college. Instead, the principal of our school told her that dropping out, with no other opportunities lined up, sounded like a good idea. She wasn't well liked at the school, so no one tried to stop her. She never even took the ACT to see if she would get scholarships for that. And she's far from the only one. Our class was pretty big, and the number actually graduating just keeps going down.

But I'm graduating. If it's the last thing I do here at this school, I'm graduating. I refuse to be sucked back in this cycle of poverty. So what if I end up being the only one, or that even my best friend couldn't make it with me. I've always been a fighter. I can keep it up for a few more months.

The Moonlighters
Brianna

"I'm happy I'm naturally smart, but as far as like managing time with my work responsibility, it's not even realistic to study when I have to do this stuff. I have to work for my family."

We caught up with Brianna, from the earlier roundtable, a few weeks after we visited her school. We talked with her more about school, work, and her family.

• • •

I just heard that I got accepted into a few colleges. I can't wait to graduate. I've decided to go to University of Louisville. They sent me a little mail about what I have to do, but I'm still waiting to see if I can get a track scholarship. For now I have my KEES and the scholarship money that I've gotten so far. I will also probably look into a few more scholarships.

Work is, ugh, stressful. I literally work all of the time. I work weekly, between thirty-two to forty hours. My mom is more stable now than she was before, so all I have to do is give her one hundred dollars a month, and it will be fine. I have been working about thirty-eight hours a week since my first job when I was about sixteen. I take care of my brother, and I help co-raise my sister. But we all help out. And my mom, she's pregnant and is due in like four weeks. That means that I will have to run everything in the house. I've always been a mom.

I can't stay after school and get help because after school, I have track or work. There is no extra support. I'm happy I'm naturally smart, but as far as like managing time with my work responsibility, it's not even realistic to study when I have to do this stuff. I have to work for my family. Plus, I don't want to spend too much time at school anyway. People there always get me in trouble.

Recently, my best friend, she's a bigger girl and black like me, had like a big argument with another girl. Since me and her look alike, they accused me of it. I was in the principal's office all day until they finally realized that I had nothing to even do with the argument. And it really made me mad that just because I look like her, I was going to get in trouble. And I told them! I was like, "You guys do realize you're punishing me for someone else!" No one was even listening to me.

Next time teachers don't know, they shouldn't go off of "I think" or "I saw." And that is part of my credibility because I'm the student and they're the teachers; I'm wrong, and they are correct. And the disciplinary actions don't matter now, because the principals are used to having a lot of kids. I mean they did realize it wasn't me and I didn't get in trouble, but I would have if I hadn't spoken up for myself. I didn't let go until they found out the truth. The teacher that was actually there finally told them that it wasn't me: "It was not her; she had nothing to do with it." Afterwards, they let me go, and I was like, "By the way, you can't punish me for looking like someone else."

I think the disciplinary thing was pretty messed up. I have one teacher that's not the best English speaker, and we don't really understand each other well. We don't communicate. But anyone who talks about him will go to an in-school suspension. It's ridiculous. Anyone that's having a hard time or has a problem, they immediately face an in-school suspension. That's his solution. It's not fair that I have to miss the rest of school, and one of the two classes that are important to me, because the teacher just doesn't understand me. Literally, the teacher just doesn't understand what I'm saying.

For example, yesterday, I told a teacher that if we're going to have a project in class, why not tell us the day before so we can bring our flash drives and everything, all of our equipment? Students kept forgetting them at home, and I knew it was an issue with an easy solution. So I was like, "Why don't you tell us the day before and then we can make sure we're prepared?" He said, "Well it's your responsibility," and I said, "Well, I agree, and I will get my work done. But if we're going to have time in class to do it, can you tell us ahead of time, so maybe we will be prepared?" I wasn't yelling or screaming, just trying to have a civil discussion. He pulled me out of the room, called the principal, and dismissed me from class.

Another time, I was a teacher's aid. After Christmas break, the teacher quit, and another teacher came in as a replacement. As the teacher's aid, I tried to tell the new replacement how class had been run for the first semester. I explained how that class required each student to sit with a computer, and I told him how the principal usually does "walk-ins" to see if classes are going smoothly. Then I proceeded to sit at my desk next to his. He was really flustered and was like, "No! You need to sit at a computer!" I tried telling him that I wasn't a student in the class, and was supposed to help him, not be enrolled. I was trying to be helpful because the old teacher had me for two years. I knew the content that was supposed to be taught, what resources we had, that kind of thing. I suppose the new setting may have been intimidating, but after telling him several times that I was not supposed to sit at the computer and take the class, I was sent to the office.

Sometimes though—rarely—I agree with the teachers. The kids can be loud sometimes. I always tell them it's annoying because it's not okay that I get taken out of the rest of my classes. But long story short, we have communication problems in this school.

On another note, I think the ACT is full of crap. I hate the reading and English sections. How are you college ready based only on your ACT score? I have gotten A's and B's my whole life. I'm a really smart kid, and I have always been top ten in my class for my whole high school career.

All year, I've been getting all A's, but this quarter specifically, I have two B's. But I got a twenty on my ACT. I don't test well, and my teachers know I have test anxiety, so every time I always do extra credit to bring my test scores up in class. I have really bad test anxiety. I sweat, I freak out. I don't feel that should measure if we're college ready. I feel like they should use your grades and how well you write in class. I think they should let teachers write you a letter of recommendation. I don't think it should be only your ACT score.

I feel like the ACT is too big of a deal. It's not that fair, and it freaks kids out. I think it stops kids from wanting to go to college. They take the ACT and they freak out about it, and it's so hard and so scary. They think that they don't have what it takes just because of a test. I had a chance to see a college and experience it. College is really hard, but through a summer program called GEAR UP Academy, I have had a few chances to live in a college dorm. It was really hard and it was stressful, but it was not that bad. It's just like high school with more freedom and harder classes. That's the only thing I could describe it as.

The ACT psyches people out, I don't think it's like a good transition at all. I don't think it's fair to take a big test, and be like, "Here, now you're ready for college." I feel like I have been working for the last twelve years, and that should count for me to go to college, not just me taking a test. And we've been preparing for twelve years. I've been preparing at home by making food for my family. I've been preparing by practicing responsibility at my difficult job. I've been getting ready in so many more ways than just a test. The test stresses me out; I hate the whole process.

I've taken the ACT four or five times, and I've studied a lot in between them with prep books. My scores went down. They have not went over twenty.

The most annoying thing about it is that I have to pay for it myself. The school provides it once or twice, but the rest is out of my own pocket. I want to take it one more time, but I don't have money for that.

I'm nervous about being broke, being poor, having no money. I don't want to end up like my parents. As of right now, I am trying to save up and praying for scholarships to come up. Like really that will fall out of the sky. If it doesn't happen? Then I won't be able to go to Louisville. I will go to Northern Kentucky University instead because I can afford it with their scholarships. I haven't saved a lot, but some. I haven't put a dent in anything.

My mom definitely wants me to go to college, but she can't help at all. Like in no way, shape, or form. She can't help me financially.

She did go back to college though. She went back to school, after I was in like sixth grade. I'm figuring out the application process myself. It's not that bad. Scholarships are hard. But I just recently reached out to my counselor, and she helped me figure out local scholarships that I qualify for. That's the hardest part, honestly. It is just the scholarships, just applying to them.

My counselor didn't really help that much. I did it myself mostly. I kind of figured it out myself. Because I went to the GEAR UP Academy, and they had a practice application class. They taught us how to apply to colleges, so I learned how to do that over the summer.

I was actually helping other students. Some of them didn't even try until I came over to help them. I would be like, "Hey, did you sign up for college?" and they said no because they didn't know how to. I had to sit down and show them. Because it's so hard, and they can't figure it out, they just don't do it.

Some of my friends want to do cosmetology. Some of them don't want to go to college at all and just want to work for the rest of their lives because applying is so hard on them. It freaks them out.

The Moonlighters
Suzie

"I can't let my grades slip because my eleven siblings are looking up to me. It gets hard to manage."

In middle school, whenever I was staying with my siblings, it was really hard. That is where most of my troubles really began.

I raised them. In middle school, my mom was taken away from me. We were separated, and that caused me to lose track of my education for a while. I was distressed and unmotivated, and I was focused on helping my siblings. I was always there with them, and I don't get to see them that often at all, like once a month. I'm adopted, so it kinda sucks, but I use that for fuel. I take a second to step out of my situation and look at the end result. I'm graduating high school and about to go to college. My next step is college. So, I need to make it through college, and I need to show them that they can do it. I need to be their example. Everything that I do is for my siblings. Because I am one of the people who didn't have parents that go to college, I have to be the person who gets out and shows people that you can be different. Like my grandma went to college. It's good to be different.

I have eleven siblings. I don't have any full siblings, they're all half siblings. I don't live with any of them. I don't see many of them often. I have my sister, but I don't get to see them in general. Like my sister, she will be a sophomore in high school, and she lives in my town with my dad. Some live thirty minutes away. Some live two hours away. Some live four hours away. So it all depends. I'm closest with my sister that lives in the town that I live in, so that's going to be the hardest to leave, but it works out in the end.

It may not be what I want it to be, but I still have the option. I still have people surrounding me that are supportive. They understand that sometimes school isn't my number one priority. I have to check in on my family, make sure that they are alright, keep everyone in check. I can't let my grades slip because my eleven siblings are looking up to me. It gets hard to manage.

I haven't had very many people to look up to, but the most important person was my undergraduate counselor that helped high school students get into college. He's always used his story to help others, and I wanna be that person one day. Him sharing his life and what helped him get through things showed me that, if I just use what I have and push through and use it as a building block instead of an obstacle, then I can get far and use that to help others get through whatever they're going through. No one is perfect and has the perfect life, and it may not be the same thing that you're going through, but they're all going through something.

He got more personal than teachers do. Most teachers in my school they were supportive, but they never went past the education. And it's definitely more than just education. You have to use your own life; sometimes barriers in your life keep you from being successful, and that's also your own decision. To have people who know and who have been in some of the same situations or have dealt with them in the same way that you have is to your advantage—especially educationally—because that feeds my life. My personal life gets in the way of my education sometimes, and I have to step back and be like, "No."

I like that my school has a lot to offer, like giving us the option to have college classes with actual professors coming to our school. That's amazing. I love that opportunity. For example, we had the option to go through our own community college, and that's mostly after school, and do dual credit courses. We're actually doing something different. We're taking away most of the AP courses, which are based on a final test that determines if you get the credit for college. And we're trying to take it more to dual credit so we can still get the college credit, and it's not based off of one final exam, it's all cumulative.

One thing I don't like about my school is that now that we are advancing in technology, they're giving all of the young kids computers. The program first started with my freshman class, and there was no problem because we were doing really good things with presentation-based learning. It was so amazing. But the problem is that we're leaning more—too much—on technology. They're letting the computer teach the child. I don't learn from computers; I learn from a person. I mean I can do it for a little bit, but I need to have a teacher. I actually ask questions. If I don't understand, I'm going to ask you. So I need a physical person to be there to know that they know what they're talking about and that I am going to be prepared in any subject matter.

Through high school, I've come to realize that you're allowed to fail. You're allowed to have a moment to not be okay, but you have to get up at some point. You have to say that it's okay not to be okay, but not all the time. In middle school, I spent a lot of time feeling sorry for myself and my mother. You have to step out of your situation no matter what and get people who build you up. Then you need to be like, "This is my education and if I want to be anywhere in life, I have to make sure that I get my life together." For other people around you, I know that there are people they look up to for support or someone that they know that looks up to them. So take that, and education is most of the way out. Some people can go straight into a job after high school, but the majority of people now have to at least have some type of degree, no matter what. So push yourself.

There have been times where I thought I couldn't make it. Oh, definitely, I felt hopeless in a lot of situations. Middle school was a big thing, and I fell off. Then freshman year came, and I didn't try. After I got through the first month or two, I was like, oh my goodness! I need to actively get my life together because I know that this is just temporary, but my grades aren't temporary. It's gonna show later on because freshman year can hurt you.

The thing that personally made this idea click was the teachers. It was the hardest class that I thought I would ever take in my life. I was struggling so much my freshman year because there's a transition from middle to high school, much like there's a transition from high school to college. But it was the people who were like "Suzie, you did better. You know you do well in this subject, so what's the problem? Why aren't you trying harder? You're just sitting in this pool of a mess; you're not contributing. You're not doing anything to better yourself, and you've always tried to, so what's different now?"

And it was that kind of wake up call from other people for me to reanalyze and be like, *Oh, this is something that I need to fix.*

I took the ACT eight times. The highest score I've ever gotten is a twenty-one. I got a nineteen three times, a twenty-one twice, and I don't really remember the rest. I would study the ACT books, but I didn't have money to go to an ACT prep course. All of my work money was going to help my family or pay house bills. Most of the money that I did get to spend on myself just went to saving up for the ACT, so I could take it again. And I tried. I feel like every time that I tried to study, like I would study for a test with the books, I just did worse. And it's weird because I did test better on English and reading than I did in science and math. But math, I've never been good at math. Science is my best subject. I love science, and I'm even going into nursing in college so it doesn't make any sense. So I just didn't understand why I didn't test well. The ACT doesn't measure you on what you know; it measures how you test.

My friend got a thirty-five, she took it four times, and the only reason she retook it after getting a thirty was because she wanted to get higher. She doesn't study or really have to try because high school is easy for her. But she knows when she gets to college, that it's going to be a big wakeup call because she's never had to study.

The ACT does not prepare me for anything. Definitely soft skills too; you don't learn any of that from the ACT. You have to learn that by living life and being your own person. Speaking, that's a big thing about it too. But I think the ACT sets people like me up for failure. I have to take a remedial math course in college because my ACT math score is a twenty. But, I have to pay for that out of my money, and I don't get credit for it. I don't think it actually accurately measures my college readiness. I don't think the ACT should be that big of an influencer, especially with money. If they just went on my GPA and not my ACT, then I could have gotten more money for college.

I'm excited about my next steps in life. I'm really excited about getting out of my little old town in Kentucky. I'm excited about being in a bigger city and being around a whole different group of people. The University of Louisville's campus is extremely diverse, and I've never been around that. I'm excited that I have the opportunity to be a leader.

I'm still going to be working—a lot. Some of the money will be used for my tuition, but most of it will be for my family. I'm not the only one to go from my county to Louisville, but I think it's unusual for people to venture too far from home. A lot of people go to community college and can transfer out, but a lot of people just stay and they're like, "I'm gonna take a year off," and then they don't go back to school.

Sometimes it's good to get away. Sometimes it's good to grow up because I know that I, for me personally, I'm kind of over that fence, but I don't think I'm gonna totally grow up until I get away and explore the real world.

Part Five
The Newcomers

Kentucky schools are seeing a significant increase in the number of immigrant and refugee students. There are over twenty-six thousand students speaking over 130 different languages in Kentucky schools.* A vast majority receive Kentucky's English Learning services, which are offered in seventy school districts spanning the Commonwealth.† While documented refugees are resettled throughout the state, Louisville resettles the bulk: sixty-one percent of the state's 2,048 documented refugees moved there in 2016.‡

For these students, high school and the college preparation process present challenges that are considerably different from those faced by others in their schools. Their distinct cultural backgrounds often make them feel like outsiders. Some may already be able to speak English fluently, but others may struggle to be understood. And if that weren't enough, political polarization around immigration casts an additional shadow over their daily lives.

They are the Newcomers.

Despite it all, these students are grateful for a chance to go to school in America. For them, education here represents hope to improve their lives and those of their families.

We would be remiss to exclude the unique perspectives of the Newcomers, students who are just as much a part of our schools as their native peers.

The Newcomers
Dhonu, David, Maaria & Sal

"After coming to America, I realized that we're unwanted by some of the people living here, especially at school."

We sat down with these students, all born in different countries, a few months after the 2016 presidential election. We spoke with them as other students from the general population convened in a different roundtable in another corner of the room. We were struck immediately by the contrast in tone: while the native-born students kept breaking out in laughter, these students were somber and serious. They had been through a lot on their journey better education opportunities.

. . .

Student Voice Team: What do you think the purpose of a postsecondary education is, and why do you think it's important or unimportant?

David: I think it's important because it allows you to move at least a step up the social ladder.

Sal: When you're in postsecondary education, you're making connections and figuring out what you want later in life.

SVT: How many of you all plan on going to college?

David: We all plan to. Like we want to.

SVT: So all of you guys plan on going to college. Why do you guys think that is? Fifty-five percent of students at this school are designated as college ready. That's not a lot. Why are you guys particularly interested in going to college?

Dhonu: More doors, opportunities.

David: We're immigrants, so the only way for us to make it here is through education. If we don't get it, we'll just get dropped down. We'll just end up like everybody else. If you get an education, that means you get to become a better person. A better life than our parents.

SVT: How long have you lived in Kentucky, and where are you originally from?

Maaria: I've lived here in Louisville for five years, I moved here from Botswana, but I'm originally from Rwanda.

David: I've been here for one and a half years, and I'm from India.

Dhonu: I'm from Nepal, I've been here for eight years, but I came from Kuwait.

Sal: I've been here in Kentucky for eight years, too. My parents immigrated from Mexico, and I was born in California after they met there.

SVT: What brought you or your families to the US?

Sal: Better life.

David: Better education and opportunity.

Maaria: My family was being relocated as refugees in Botswana, and the US was taking refugees, so we were relocated to here.

David: We were refugees, too. So we signed and everything, and we went through the process, and they brought us here.

Sal: I'd say more economic stability.

SVT: Does anyone feel comfortable sharing their family's journey or how they got here to the US?

Sal: My parents are both from Mexico. They both came to the US to work and make more money, to help their parents and their families out in Mexico. They originally planned to work for a certain amount of time and then go back to Mexico whenever they were able to build a base to live off of. But it's just so much better here in the United States, because what you can make here in two days you would make in one week over there. So they ended up meeting each other here at a factory that they worked in, and they got together, and then I came along, so they stayed here. We lived in Santa Ana, California, for a long time. It got to the point where it was hard for them to keep or find a job, so we decided to move here to Kentucky, and since we've moved here it's gotten a lot better.

Dhonu: We lived in a refugee camp, so I would say it was harsh. I had a disabled brother, and my father had to go out of the country for work, so he would stay there for about a year and send money back and come back for a month and then go back again. And when we heard about the International Organization for Migration (IOM) and how they were sending people to America, we signed up for it, and we had to go through a process. They did medical tests, background tests, everything. And then when we came here, it was different. We came here for a better life. Where we came from, there was nothing. They sent me out for a better education. The camp where we lived, I wouldn't say the education was bad, but we had to sit in the floor and write on a piece of paper. There were no desks, no nothing. It was harsh there, and when we moved here, we had trouble with adjustments. We didn't know the language. We didn't know how the system worked and everything, but as we got used to it, it got better.

David: Basically, we moved from India because of my education. Everything was fine, economically and everything. If we want to have a better education, like if I wanted to go to medical school in India, it cost too much money. And we don't get any help from the government like we do over here, like FAFSA and scholarships. So we have to come out of pocket. We could not afford it. The other thing was that the education system in India is very different from here. It's very hard, so it's kind of depressing for students over there. It was really tough for me, so my parents decided to move over here. My uncle and my grandma were already here, so we came over here last year.

We lived in the refugee camp. My mom is from India and my dad is from Bhutan, and when I was two years old, they moved to the refugee camp because my father's family was in there. I grew up in there. After I finished tenth grade, I wanted to do something better. I wanted to go to medical school. But because of poverty, my family could not afford the education and once we heard that IOM was going to send people to America, we did everything. They checked our medical record and everything. Once we came here, it was really hard for me to learn English. I went to ESL (English as a Second Language) class. Last year, I transferred here. It was really hard for my family. Only my father worked in my family, now I have to work with my family, and I have to go to college. I really want to go to college to make my future bright.

Maaria: My family's from Rwanda. After the genocide, everything was fine, but at some point we started facing religious persecution because we're Jehovah's Witnesses. When I was really young my family moved to Tanzania. Then moved to Malawi, then to Zimbabwe, and finally Botswana. I grew up in Botswana, so that's mostly all I know. The Botswana government was resettling refugees elsewhere, so we got resettled in the US. We didn't really get to pick; it was the only option we had. We couldn't stay in Botswana, and we couldn't go anywhere else, so this was the best option. I think it took five years. Medical checks and background checks and all those.

SVT: What were your first impressions of the US when you arrived versus what they are now? What's your first language?

Maaria: At home we speak in Kinyarwanda, the official language of Rwanda. I speak five languages: Kinyarwanda, Kirundi, Swahili, Tswana, and English. When I first got here—you know how other countries think the US is all about freedom and opportunities? Yeah, I did too. But when we first came here, there's more freedom than other countries, but right now, it's not as promising as it was five years ago. Maybe because of the new presidency? But whether it is that or actually living here instead of just hearing about it, it doesn't sound or look as appealing as it was five years ago.

Dhonu: In my home, I speak Nepali and English. Once I got here, I was really worried: Do I get an education or not? My first thing was education. I wished for opportunity when I came here.

SVT: So you had more of a positive impression?

Dhonu: Yeah.

David: I speak Gujarati at home. My uncle used to say good stuff about education. "Don't worry about education. You'll always get good opportunities no matter what, and you're a good student, so you'll get into whatever you want, it's not like in India."

So I had pretty good impressions. When I came here, I didn't know much, and I was about nine years old. Getting off the plane and getting in a car for the first time, all I saw was lights. It was night when we came in. It was like five days when I couldn't find anyone to talk to, no friends, no nobody. So it was actually really depressing when I first came here and my first impression was bad.

Dhonu: As I got used to it and started making friends, it got better, and I started learning, which was even better. And right now, I really like the US because it offers education and medicine for people. When we were in Nepal, the medical aspect wasn't good. First coming in, it was bad. Now I see everything that the US offers.

Sal: At home, I speak Spanish. I was born here. We moved to Mexico for a year. One of the things I remember was how at the beginning of the school year here, you're automatically enrolled, but in Mexico you kind of had to race to get to school. I remember my mom would rush to different schools to apply because if you weren't one of the first people to apply, the spots would fill up and if you didn't make it, you didn't make it. You'd have to sit out a whole year and try to get into another school again. The education system is completely different. When I got back, it made me realize how everything was a lot better here.

SVT: And you're from an undocumented family, right?

Sal: Yeah.

SVT: What does that feel like, over the last six months?

Sal: Over the last six months, it's been tough going to school since they know my family is undocumented. Even though I'm a citizen, it makes me feel like I'm unwanted, like an outcast. I feel like I've been labeled as an "anchor baby," and I don't know how I feel about that because behind that term is the meaning that my parents used me as a way of staying in this country, but I don't think that's the case at all.

SVT: Do you have thoughts about what you've been hearing politically or from people in school?

Maaria: These days, foreigners are labeled, especially if they're from North Africa or somewhere close to the Middle East, you're kind of labeled as a terrorist, but not really. In the travel ban, they stop some African countries from entering the US. So when people hear about African countries which are banned, they think the automatic issue is the whole of Africa, they're all terrorists like the ones who are banned. Being labeled that way makes you feel like you're not getting what you expected.

SVT: What is it like being an immigrant or refugee as a student? What is it like being new in a place?

David: I like the education system here, and I like the way things run. As a student, I appreciate the opportunities I've been opened to, especially as an immigrant, since I didn't have the fortunes back home. Now I do. I've learned to appreciate it. The bad part of it is that people don't seem to understand what an immigrant is. They assume you came in illegally and tried to take over what others already have. They need to know that immigrants come here legally and have had background checks done for a long time. It's good here, but it's bad being misunderstood.

SVT: And how does that affect your education? Do you feel like it's difficult at first?

Maaria: When I first came here, I did ESL, and that helped me pick up a little English before I went to classes with everybody else. It's kind of hard not knowing English, but then it's a good thing because teachers try to help you through it.

Sal: The best part of the education system over here are the teachers. Teachers try to help you and get you going. The thing is that it's hard to be an immigrant student. Not in terms of education, but in terms of getting used to the things that an American student goes through. We are different from them. We have different mindsets, norms, culture. We're like the odd one out over here. I was told by one classmate that immigrants like us are stealing their opportunities and social securities.

SVT: How'd that make you feel?

Sal: I felt really mad? Sad? I was like, your government is trying to help us and I really appreciate it. I'm not illegal or undocumented, and even if I was undocumented, if this country has a power to help someone, then why don't you want to help them? I know the US has the power to help so many families over there. There are so many families dying of hunger in refugee camps. If you had a look at refugee camps in various places, you'd realize it's hard to be an immigrant. We're not here to steal your things; we just need your help.

SVT: Did you feel bullied when that person said that? What was your reaction?

Sal: I didn't feel bullied, but I felt that I wanted to know what Americans think about immigrants because I've met so many Americans and they all have different opinions. We were having class discussions, and he just kept his point of view. I didn't have issues that he kept his point of view. Maybe it's part of his way of thinking, his family, his environment, I don't know.

SVT: Was it hurtful?

Sal: Kind of. Because he wasn't thinking, he didn't know what immigrant life looked like. It's not his fault, but he should have thought before he spoke.

SVT: If there's one thing that you want American students to know, what would it be?

David: That you guys are great, that you're allowing us to share your things. But don't treat us like we're unwanted. We're here because we need help, and it's really nice that you guys are allowing us to be part of your family because immigrant life isn't easy. When you're an immigrant, you're not part of your country or the country that you're in. When I go back to India, they'll be like, "You're American now. You don't belong here." And when I'm here, they're like, "You're Indian. You don't belong here." So we're of nowhere, and it's really hard to be an immigrant.

Dhonu: When you're an immigrant, you feel odd because you do things weird. You're living a way of life that people aren't used to. So they see you as an outcast. If they don't, it's seen as very odd, the things you're doing, the way you are, the way you dress, even. And the education system and everything, I'm very grateful for it. There are people still stuck in my country who don't have the same opportunities as me. That's why I was striving for postsecondary education. I don't know. I've been able to experience education in two different countries, so I know how many more opportunities you get here than in other countries.

SVT: What about the teachers or what you're learning in school here? Is that similar?

Sal: One thing that I've become aware of is the way that teachers here in the United States make money. They make a pretty good amount. In other countries, like in Latin America, it's pretty bad. Teachers don't get paid very well, so there isn't that drive, even if they want to help students. It's like, if I do this, I won't be able to provide for myself or live a comfortable lifestyle. I'd say, because of that, teachers and other school-related jobs aren't as good as they are here.

SVT: Has it ever affected your academic performance, being called names, being bullied, being treated unfairly? Do you ever feel like it's made it more difficult to study or work on your education?

Maaria: When you first move here and you speak another language or you have a thick accent, they just drop you into the ESL class to learn English. And then they just drop you into the honors classes, and that's about it. When I first got here, I hadn't known that AP classes or advanced classes existed. If I had known, I'd have tried to take them earlier. When I came here, I wasn't told anything about them. I found out about them for myself in junior year, and that's when I started taking them. But for other students who came in as immigrants and didn't find out, they are forced to stay in lower classes that don't do them any justice. Some are really intelligent students who would do really well in AP classes, but they never knew about them, no one ever told them about them, so they don't have AP classes on their high school transcript which won't look as good on their college application.

SVT: We were speaking with a Chinese student, and she said her ESL class was almost completely geared towards Spanish students, and no one spoke Mandarin to her, and she was confused for her first week, her first time in America. I assume that they didn't speak Swahili, or any of the other languages that you know, in ESL classes, or maybe they did. So what was your experience in ESL?

Maaria: The kids in ESL were from all over the world, and almost none of them spoke the Scotte language, the language I speak. But the teacher who teaches doesn't speak any other language except English. They try to make you understand, but if you don't speak even a tiny bit of English, that's not good. But here in Louisville, they have a school called ESL Newcomers Academy, and if you don't speak even a little bit of English, you go there, and then you get transferred to a different school.

SVT: If you could change one thing about ESL, what would it be?

Dhonu: For my school, they had just one Nepali teacher. I'd try to get other teachers who speak different languages instead of focusing only Nepali students to the Nepali teacher. I think that would have helped, because in my other classes, it was kind of hard to understand what was going on with it being a different language and a different subject. So if I had a teacher who spoke my language, it could have been easier.

SVT: And you talked about how you had to find those AP classes for yourself. Do you feel like there's anyone in the school who's looking out for you?

Sal: I found out about AP and advanced classes from a friend who was here before me, and I spoke to a teacher called Mr. Peters. He was really good about helping me and other students, so I feel like he's one of the teachers who actually does look out for me the most. He's the one who encouraged me to take AP classes. If it wasn't for him, I don't think I would have

Maaria: When I came here, I didn't have any knowledge about this situation, and how this education system worked, so I was just given one schedule and there was one senior girl who showed me my classes. After that, I had no clue where I should go or who I should talk with. There was this place in ESL class; I didn't even know it was an ESL class, that I just went to my next class and I struggled in every class. In my government class, my teacher didn't tell me anything. I came in the middle of the year, so I missed a lot of stuff, so I didn't even know what to do. She just handed me an assignment and was like, "You're supposed to do that." But what about that? I didn't know anything. I had a really hard time and had to figure out everything by myself. I had to go to the counselor every day, and she tried to help me, but I think that help wasn't enough. I talked to some of my friends that were out of the school, and they tried to help me. They told me about AP classes, the ACT. I hadn't known I had to take the ACT for placement, and I hadn't known how important it was. I struggled a lot when I got here. But the good thing is that I got some teachers who really cared about me, like Mr. Peters. He's the one who always helped me and tried to make me comfortable.

Dhonu: I came here in 2008 and there wasn't much of a Nepali population here, so they didn't really know how to deal with Nepali kids. You said it was more geared towards Spanish-speaking kids, and it was kind of like that when I first came here because there were a lot of Spanish immigrants. My ESL class was full of Hispanics, so it was geared towards them. But at the school I went to, the teacher was really good, so she helped me through it.

SVT: Were you scared that the students wouldn't accept you, that the teachers wouldn't accept you? What was preventing you from being accepted?

Maria: I felt like I wouldn't be accepted by my classmates, and at the same time, I felt like my teachers didn't think I was capable of that kind of work.

SVT: Why did they think you weren't capable?

Maria: Well, that was what I thought. Nobody ever told me and was like, "You shouldn't be in these classes because you're not smart enough." In fact, I had a few teachers who would recommend me being in AP or advanced classes, but I just never wanted to because of the mentality that I had. For me, it took that extra push that I got from Coach T. Pushing myself and trying to block all that other stuff out was the main thing for me.

SVT: What do you hope to get out of school and what do you hope to do in the future?

Sal: I want to go to college so I can get a good job and be able to make money, so I can take care of my parents, because if they stay here, well, whatever they decide to do, if they go back to Mexico, they won't have anything because they've been working here their whole life. And they can't retire or get retirement money or anything like that. So I feel like it's up to me to look after them when they can't work anymore.

SVT: Where do you want to be ten, twenty years from now?

Sal: I don't know. I've already been accepted into college, but I don't know what I want to study. I've thought about it a lot, but I just don't know.

David: I want to pursue my education and get a degree in either medicine or business; I'm still figuring this out. The reason for that is to have a better life, obviously.

Maaria: After graduating from high school, I'm going to college, to U of L, and after that I want to go to med school.

Dhonu: After high school I'm going to Centre College to study either medicine or business. I feel like it's my duty to take care of my parents because they're immigrants and they're not educated. Getting an education will be a way to take care of my parents.

SVT: What is your family's view towards college?

Sal: I have to go to college, because that was one of the big reasons we came here, to have a better education and a better life. College is a gate to a better life, that's how they see it.

David: Both my parents encourage me to stay in school and go to college, mainly because they know that through education, I'll be able to live a better life than they did.

Dhonu: My parents care a lot; they want me to go to college and have a better life.

Maaria: My family values education, and I've learned to value it too. And if I were to mention anything about not going to college, I think I'd be kicked out of the house. When I came over here, I was hoping for so much and had a really good image of America. But after coming to America, I realized that we're unwanted by some of the people living here, especially at school. It feels like someone has slapped me in the face and reminded me that my daydreams about America were nothing more than dreams, and the reality is a nightmare. But we are working hard. Our voices won't be silent forever.

The Newcomers
Zainab & Imani

"I don't know about the college, but the high school is not as competitive as it is in my country."

We had first met these students when we visited their after-school program in a Louisville neighborhood that was a center for refugee resettlement. With all the headlines about America's shifting immigration policies in early 2017, we wanted to learn more about how students from marginalized communities were being affected and share some of our student voice research about how they might ensure they are better heard in their school systems. This second encounter was supposed to be more focused around the issue of college readiness, but it quickly became a conversation about so much more.

. . .

Student Voice Team: Where are you guys from? How long have you been here?

Zainab: I'm originally from Pakistan, and I have been in the United States for two and a half years.

Imani: I'm from East Africa and I have been here for one and a half years.

SVT: Can you explain the process of getting here?

Zainab: My dad worked on a ship. He was a seaman, and he visited many different countries, but my mom wanted him to go to the United States. So my dad lived here for eight years and then worked so he could invite us. Our living conditions in Pakistan weren't good, and we were supposed to pay for everything in our education. Also, it was really dangerous because of the Taliban. They banned our schools—we were not allowed to go. Especially girls, because they say that girls are only for marrying, having kids, and staying in the house.

Imani: As I said, I am from East Africa, and my parents were from the Congo. I was born in a different country. Life there was very difficult for them. I am very lucky.

SVT: How long did it take?

Zainab: Our case was rejected three times. They rejected my dad the first time, then they rejected him again, and then he went to talk to a senator from Kentucky. He told him that he couldn't afford anything because all the money he made here, he sent it to us for our education.

Imani: The US tightened the process for people arriving from the Congo, so we applied through a program in Africa. We were accepted and sent an invitation to come visit.

SVT: How easy was the process?

Imani: I think it was quite easy for me, but for other people it's harder because they ask you lots of questions. They ask how you fled from the Congo, what you plan to do, and other things. They didn't ask me anything because I didn't know what they wanted to know, and I was younger than most.

Zainab: It was really hard, and it is getting more dangerous there because there is no freedom. If you're not following the Taliban and doing what they say, they will shoot and kill you. So we waited for maybe four to five years. My mom was always worried about us because when she sent us to school, she didn't know if we were going to come back home or not.

SVT: What was your impression of America when you first came here?

Zainab: I was very surprised! The environment, the people. I never saw people open and independent. In my neighborhood, we had hardly any technology. It was really hard to get. Here, every single person, every kid had cell phones, and they can even use it in school. In my school in Pakistan, if they saw you using a cell phone, they would call your parents, and you would be out of school for three days.

Imani: For me, it was technology and education. Back there, it was hard to get education. I just came with a book to study. Here, I can get all of the education I want.

Zainab: The country was so different for me, you know? Like a culture shock. In my country, there was a park near the Taliban, and they were bombing it and all of that. For me, it seemed really secure here.

SVT: How was the transition of you going to school here? Was it hard or easy taking the classes?

Zainab: For me, I think the study is very easier than in my country. In my country, it is very competitive and even my teachers would say, "You are making it so hard for yourself! A woman like you shouldn't study! Don't waste your time doing this when you could just be a wife." Now in my class in the United States, people look at me funny when I participate. I'm not saying that I'm the smartest kid, but whenever a teacher ask a question, I raise my hand. I'm like, "Oh my gosh, I already learned this stuff!" Whatever the teachers are teaching now, they taught us in ninth grade. The education system I think is very easy, not competitive. Kids here haven't seen competitive. I don't know about the college, but the high school is not as competitive as it is in my country. In my country if you don't have good grades, you aren't going to go on another year to the next level. I used to study until like 2:00 a.m. in the morning and would only sleep like three hours every single night.

Imani: It was hard to me. I didn't know anybody from the school, but once I met someone who spoke the same language as me, I was able to do something that was challenging, and that's how the school comes together. Wait, that's not what I mean. That's how the school comes easy to me. They helped me to do something. I already know a lot of what is being taught in math, but I cannot show it. It was nice to have a friend.

SVT: So what grade did you learn some of the material you are being taught now?

Imani: Like sophomore year—well, I skipped sophomore year. They tested me in math and English. Once I passed the test, they told me I was going to be a junior instead of a sophomore.

SVT: Wow! So when you came here, did you already learn English back in your country, so it was easy to get here because you already had that experience?

Zainab: Yes, the school I used to go to was an army-based school. It was very hard. We had to pay double because we were not children of the army. We were civilians. And my mom, she really didn't want us to go to public school, because in public school they don't teach you English. Well, they teach you English, but it's only like common words. So I used to go to the army school, and I used to say that my dad used to send money and my mom had to pay double for our education. It was very hard. There was no public bus. There was no free books like we have here. They give you books in class, but you have to buy them with your own money. You have to buy every single thing by your own self.

Imani: When I was little, it was in English. But the English is different from the USA, it was British English. Sometimes you can say something and they cannot get what you say, but if you write it down, it is easier. English was very hard.

SVT: Did you all have school books, too?

Imani: No, you gotta buy them.

SVT: Did you use calculators?

Imani: Sometimes. For me they were very hard to use. It took me the most time.

SVT: How does your family feel about you going to college? What do they think about college? How do they support you?

Zainab: My mom, she gives importance to education because she is uneducated. She thinks that if we don't get educated, it will cause a lot of problems for us: the hardships of just working like a normal job. She wants us to have a comfortable life. She is so sick here, but she never tried to show us that she was sick. If she did, she knew it would have an effect on our education. We would be depressed about it, and then we couldn't do well in school. She really fought hard for us, even though she said she had a heart problem. She is the one that is motivating me a lot. She is my inspiration. She always, in every single thing of my life, she supports me. My dad do the same, but not as my mom. He tries to be so honest. You know my dad, he provided me everything. But my mom, even when she was not making money, she would do teller work. You know, like sewing? So when someone says something about my mom in school, how she is odd, I never say anything back to them. It makes me so mad. Right now, ACT is coming, she said even if you don't get a perfect score—I know I'm not going to get a perfect score. It's hard for me to get good in reading because it's not in my language. She said, even if you do bad, you just keep practicing so you can go to like a really good college. It's like her dream to see me as a cardiologist because she has heart problems.

Imani: They want me to go to college because I'm the oldest kid in my family. Once I graduate, I can help my mom and my younger siblings. That's the expectation they have. I can make them strong when I get into college, so I have to make sure I am focusing on my education. They want to see me do well, but they also want to know that they are taken care of, that I can look for them. I am the oldest, so I don't get much support. I have to be the man and support everyone else.

Zainab: So when I stay after school for clubs and activities, she always tell me, before you make any decisions, just think about it. How am I going to benefit from this thing? What's going to be the consequences? She said this after my time in my old school. Once there was a time when I was going to the Holocaust museum in Washington, DC, with my teacher. I was stopped in the airport because I was wearing hijab. She just like stopped me. So I got so emotional. My mom said, "Don't let yourself down because of others." I was like, "Okay, the people in school, they were like picking on me." My mom helped me through that.

SVT: Wow, your mom sounds like a really nice person. You are very lucky to have her. So how do you guys think you've been prepared for the ACT? Do you think the teachers have done really well? And what do you think about the ACT itself, in terms of getting into college?

Zainab: I think um, I'm not trying to be mean, but I'm saying that my school is preparing us for it, but it's not really helping us. Like right now, I'm going to do everything on my own. I think I am prepared for it, but I have to work really hard for it. My school hasn't really been—they just teach normal stuff, like what you want to learn. They don't teach you about the ACT. That's why it is so hard for us because we were not here in the United States at a young age. They didn't teach us.

Imani: The ACT is really hard for the people that weren't born here because they put stuff on there that hasn't been taught in the past. And second, English is our second language, so before we guess an answer and get it right, we have to translate it to our native language to make it as understandable as we can. Reading, grammar, we don't know all of those. It is not that I am not smart. I do well in my classes because I ask questions. I talk to the teacher. I get help and work hard. I could do that in college too, but the ACT doesn't show it.

SVT: So what do you think they should do to prepare you guys for the ACT?

Imani: Helping us in reading and English with grammar. The math is not as hard as the English because it's not in our second language. There's not a class in our school that is going to help you with the ACT. There are just classes you have to pass, to get to college—they are credits. So whatever we are going to do, it depends on us.

SVT: How is your relationship with other students and teachers? How would you describe that?

Zainab: When I ask a lot of questions in class or something, the other students get mad at me. I saw one time on social media that they used the hashtag #QuestionGame with a picture of me because I was asking too many questions. I'm so nice to everybody, you know? Like, I always help people. I always smile and try to be friends with them. But they say that I am a nerd. But that's why I came here! That's why I came to the United States—to get an education, to get the advantages of the opportunities they are providing. If they are getting mad at me, it's not my problem. It's not my fault. Okay, if I'm going to be quiet, then you should give answer to teacher. There's no one giving answers to teachers, I'm the only one. I think my teachers, they're the best.

Imani: Yeah I think the teachers, they do their jobs as well. The problem is the students. Sometimes they want to play, or when they ask a question about getting here, or how is the country doing. You cannot flee the country if it's good, and you would not move if you have all you need in that country. So I don't know why they keep asking the questions like that. They're just ignorant. Some they think it's funny, but it's not really.

Zainab: When people say something about me or about my religion, I never silence myself. Even if the teachers don't agree with me, I always say it. I never say it in a mean way, I just always say, "Guys, this is not the right thing." I just do the right things for me, my school, my teachers, I never become silenced. And my friends—from Muslim countries—always say, "Don't do that, they might hurt you." I'm not scared if they hurt me. I'm not scared. Malala Yousafzai once said, "If the world becomes silent only one voice can change the world." So if one person like me can go and say something, it's going to change.

SVT: For the students in your class that actually care, do they care about your education? Do they support you when you talk about college, or when you talk about your situation or your culture?

Imani: Yeah they do. Some want to know what college you want to go to, it depends on what subject you want to know.

Zainab: Last month, I was running for the class officers for senior year. I'm not popular. I think there were two girls running against me, and they were American and they were popular. Then they tore down my posters. It was disrespectful. And they were telling people, "She's an English as a Second Language. How is she going to go and talk for you?" It did make me feel so depressed. Those two weeks, I didn't eat any lunch in school. Who could care? I was depressed because they were saying things about me. Mom was mad. "What are you doing?" she'd ask. We started making index cards: "Vote Zainab for president!" Each day and each week, I go and distribute them to students at the cafeteria. It did make a difference. A lot of people, they didn't know me, but because of them, I won president.

SVT: That's amazing! Congratulations! What are you planning to do next year with these accomplishments?

Zainab: I want to go to the University of Louisville, but I'm not sure I will go. If my ACT gets like good, I will go. I want to prove other people wrong. I'm just going to make it possible. I might get in, but I won't get any money. That worries me.

SVT: Do you know how you're going to be able to pay for college? Scholarships, FAFSA?

Zainab: I always ask questions from teachers, and sometimes I talk with counselors. The thing is, I'm so worried. Like, my teachers, even my mom, they say, "Do not be too hard on yourself." But I cannot help it. It's just the way I was born. It's a nature thing. But anyways, there is a question I always ask: How am I going to pay for this? There is so much pressure on me with the finances. Like how am I going to get full tuition?

Imani: My family, they cannot afford college for me, and I don't want to put pressure on them. Because of my ability and my intelligence, I want to go to college. I just don't want to put pressure on them. They already have pressure and obstacles put on them. I read about the FAFSA. I'm not sure how it work or if I can get it, but I want to try.

Zainab: We will both try.

Imani: We will prove them wrong.

Part Six
The Oddsbuckers

On paper, these are the students who are not expected to graduate high school and pursue a postsecondary degree. But somehow, they are the same students who manage to overcome every obstacle: a culture telling them that college is not for them, limited education resources, unstable families, poor health, or shaky finances.

The Oddsbuckers are the outliers.

How do they do it, and from where does their source of self-determination come? For the students we spoke with, the answers are as varied as the students themselves.

For one student, it was his desire to be accepted as more than his disability. For another, it was her own determination, plus a counselor acting as a cheerleader, to leave the family farm to pursue her dream of becoming a nurse. And for another still, it was the pressure she felt to serve as a positive role model for her younger siblings in her parents' neglectful absence.

Stories from the Oddsbuckers bring some optimism to our understanding of student struggles with college readiness. They offer examples of how students can draw on resources around and within themselves to change their expected trajectory and take control over their own learning and lives.

The Oddsbuckers serve as living proof that data is not destiny.

The Oddsbuckers
Jordan

"Leaving this county means saying goodbye to my family because they won't want to see a traitor like me. Leaving this county is about so much more than just education."

Being deaf doesn't mean that I am mute, but people have a lot of trouble understanding that. Everyone assumes that I can only lip read, and they continue their conversations without a second thought. I wonder if they have ever tried lip reading. I bet they couldn't do it—it's really hard. I can barely do it even though I have been practicing for years. Can you look at two different objects at once? No, you can't, because it is not possible to focus on two different objects on different sides of a room. So, why do people think that I can look at several different people during a conversation, interpret what each person is saying, and sign my thoughts to my interpreter? No one thinks about how hard that is. Instead, they just assume that I am shy and don't have much to say. I like talking to you here today, though. You are actually listening to me.

I was placed in a program that focuses on deaf education because in regular classes, I missed a lot. And, no, it wasn't that I didn't understand what was happening or that I couldn't do the calculations. In fact, I'm a lot smarter than them, but I can't prove it because my interpreter doesn't always get everything. It is hard for me. I have to study more, but I have A's and B's. I might be one of the only people in my school with this situation, but I know that there are others across Kentucky that feel the same way. It's hard for people with hearing disabilities, especially in a culture that doesn't really value our education. They assume that if I "toughen up" and "stop whining" or "get thicker skin," then I will be fine. But they have to be patient with me, and I know that I have to be patient with them.

I just want to be in the real world. I need to get out of here. Everyone is the same here. Everyone knows everyone, so there's gossip and everything. I want to make some new friends and have fun with normal people: people that have traveled to places outside of this county, people that understand that while my disability exists, it doesn't define me. You will not believe the number of people here that refuse to talk to my interpreter. They think that I'm faking it.

Before all of this, I went to a school for the deaf. I would have stayed there if I could. I really loved it there. But my mom made me come back here—to the mainstream. My parents felt disconnected from my education because they didn't hear directly from the administration as much as they wanted to. Usually, I was the one updating them about my grades or classes. They didn't like that. They wanted to be more involved in my education, so they went ahead and brought me back to mainstream school. I'm mad that such a little administrative issue caused me to move schools. Now, I am stuck in a community that doesn't understand me.

I plan to go to Eastern Kentucky University (EKU). My major is going to be wildlife management. Yup. Not farming, not agriculture, not welding. Wildlife management. I'm going to be there for about four years to study it. I'm not quite sure if they have a disability center like other bigger state schools. Honestly, I didn't really look into it. I didn't even think about it. I just assumed that going to a university meant that I would be able to meet people like myself. People underestimate how important culture, belonging, and understanding are to me. So if I don't get into EKU or meet people that understand me, I'll just go to the military. That is always an option.

But see, I've already started preparing. I know how important AP classes are for college. I want to take AP classes, but I'm only in pre-AP science right now. I've focused on science to match up with my major in wildlife, but my school doesn't have very many science classes. We have a lot of classes in agriculture and farming, but that is pretty much it. Most of the learning that I do is on my own. I'll go home after school and read about forests or exotic animals after I do my homework. The homework is just busywork anyway, and no one really does it at my school in the first place. I wish I could take my wildlife books into class so that I could actually do something useful with my time. I mean, I don't talk to teachers or students anyway. I would never bring the books in, though. I don't want to be the subject of small town gossip again.

Besides classes, I've taken the ACT a few times already. I'm in the process of taking it again right now. The first time I got a seventeen, then I got an eighteen. I want to improve it because I need a higher score to get into EKU. I know that I want to attend the university this fall, but I still have to apply and get accepted. I'm sure that will happen. If I just meet benchmarks, what else could there be? That's what all of my teachers tell me. They say, "Meet benchmarks so you can be college ready!" So if all I need is an ACT score, I'll be fine in college.

I don't really know why there is such a large emphasis on the ACT. It's just a test. I think GPA is better because it shows that I'm an A/B student. I take the ACT, and it doesn't show that at all. It doesn't show what I can do. But yet again, all of the colleges want ACT scores; all of the teachers are pushing them; and, all of the counselors stress them. Maybe I'm just stupid and don't see the importance of it. The teachers and counselors know best anyway. So I'll just keep taking the ACT again, and again, and again.

My dad didn't go to college. He got his high-school diploma and works, just like most of the people here. My mom went to college. She actually works here at my school. My brothers are younger than me, so they haven't had the opportunity to look for colleges yet. I'm going to be the first in the family, of the children, to go to college. My dad is kinda laid back. He says things like, "Oh you'll be fine. You don't need college. You can just go to work like me." He is actually very offended that I want to leave home and go to college. He thinks that I feel that I am too good for my own family. I've already made up my mind, though. I need to go to college or the military. If I leave, I doubt they will let me come back to visit. Leaving this county means never seeing it again. Leaving this county means saying goodbye to my family because they won't want to see a traitor like me. Leaving this county is about so much more than just education.

One of my teachers has been amazing, and she helped me a lot when planning my future. The other teachers don't really care. I decided to go to EKU by myself. I applied, researched, and planned my entire future by myself. I'm thinking about applying to other colleges, but I'm not really sure that I will be able to manage it because the counselor is not going to help me.

The school decides if you're ready for college or a career. My goal is to go to college. I feel that the teachers at my school are more laid back and don't really teach us, but we can't get them fired. It's really frustrating for me because I want a new teacher that motivates me and helps me learn. There's not a lot of teachers here. They've always been the same teachers who teach the same things over and over. They've just gotten really complacent, so it's really hard for me to stay motivated and do more. This county is more focused on agriculture and farming; they don't really care for higher education. The students just want to graduate high school and work on a farm and have a basic life. They do what they have to do. The teachers don't really try because they know that the students just want to be farmers. So if you want a real education, well, we don't have that here.

My parents aren't interested in giving me advice or being a part of the college search process. They were only a little involved in high school. My family is pressuring me to go to work instead of college, but I really want to go to college. I want to get a master's degree. That's my ultimate goal. Man is that good money. Maybe if I come back rich my family will like me again, or maybe that will make the situation even worse.

Most of my friends want to go to college. That's why I hang out with them. None of us really know what we are doing so we try to help each other out. My best friend also wants to go to EKU, so it is helpful to have him. Like me, he wants to major in something that isn't really taught in school. He likes photography and stuff like that. If there was an entire school of students like him, I probably wouldn't leave.

Some of my friends don't care. My teachers don't care. My parents don't even care about my education. I wouldn't leave if I felt like I had another option. I need to break free because I feel that there is something or some place for me outside of this county. People might call me odd for believing that there is a life outside of this small town, but I keep hoping. That's all we have sometimes.

The Oddsbuckers
Akhil

"State loyalty is valued, but I'm like, 'If you're getting better opportunities elsewhere, why would you not take them?'"

Okay, so I know college and career readiness is something that a lot of schools are going for right now, but I think a lot of times, the way we see college readiness doesn't have anything to do with college. I think sometimes the state pushes taking ACT's and classes that are supposed to be like "college prep." But that's not, in reality, helping you at all for college. If I've figured out one thing, you need to learn how to do things for yourself. Most times, they tell students, "We're going to force you to take this test," instead of encouraging you. No one's really there to encourage you, and sometimes, college may not be the right path for you.

Sometimes I think it's just a big umbrella term that they use to act like they're doing something when they're not doing anything. I think a lot of times, smaller organizations like scholarship committees and private organizations are doing more work than entire high schools. When I was applying to college, it wasn't my school that led me; it was individual people. I think my teachers and counselor were the most influential. It wasn't like some state-guided program. Those didn't help me at all. Like the ILP (Individual Learning Plan) that didn't help me in any way, but it's one of those things that's meant to "help you get ready for college." And it's not. I was told I should be a locksmith for like six years in a row, and I'm pretty sure I'm not going to become a locksmith.

At my high school, there's lots of really good teachers, and there's lots of very bad teachers. And that's assumed at any high school, but I felt like there was a group of three teachers who were always there for me. They were like my three moms. They helped me through junior year. That third year hits, and you get like insane amounts of homework. Junior year, I had five AP tests, and if anything taught me how to study, it was those. Three of them were practically self-study. One of them was actually self-study, but the other two were because that teacher, well, you know what I mean. But then, going to senior year, that's when it really matters that you have those connections with teachers.

I think a lot of times when students are going to college or doing applications and stuff, and they kind of get lost, it's because they don't have teachers who they really made connections with. This is going to sound a little bit pretentious, but it's a lot easier for people to apply in state because they have people to look up to. They have people to tell them what it's like. For instance, when I was applying to Yale, I literally had no one to read my application and tell me if it was good. I don't know what college was looking for because I don't know anyone who's ever gotten into a place like that.

I got a "likely letter" from Brown. It was really exciting. It was really funny that day. I was wearing my Brown sweatshirt, and I walked home and thought, *Wait, why was there a letter?* All of the decisions for college were supposed to be released March 31, but I knew colleges sent likely letters to people who they really, really want. Then I wondered, *Why is Brown sending me a letter?* And I open it up, and it read, "You have been granted admission, but we can't give you the official thing until the thirty-first." And I literally, like, died. I was in shock.

I think a lot of the top of the class do find teachers whom they connect with. There are some people who are not necessarily the top ten of the class, but they are still able to find their teachers who they really like. I think it's important to remember that teachers are people too; you can connect with them. You can talk to them. I think a lot of times, people just avoid them, and that is something that students need to work on. I think teachers are very welcoming in that sense, especially in rural communities. These schools are community centered. But with only fifty students per grade, people just refuse to talk to teachers, and I think that's when they start falling behind in terms of applying to college or going after high school. You need adults in your life other than your parents to help you out.

Yeah, so I also got into Yale, University of Chicago (U Chicago), NYU (New York University), and USC; I got rejected from Princeton and Stanford; and waitlisted at Harvard and Columbia. But it didn't matter because I wanted to go to Yale anyway.

After I opened the Yale portal I was like, *Do I even want to open the Princeton portal?* I did anyway, and then I was rejected, and I was like, *Awkward.* I think there was a severe lack of resources and connections to basically anywhere out of state. It's not even elite universities. There's no one who went to NYU, or if you're looking at USC, there's still no one there.

I think there's always a huge divide between the students who are advanced and those who are not, especially in smaller schools. I'm only friends with the top five of the class really. I think a lot of times, it's like self selection. You're always wanting to choose the most intelligent people around you. So school divides are natural, and I think in society, we divide ourselves with people who are like us, who are interested in actually doing something with their life as opposed to just sitting.

A dual diploma program really split my class. There was only forty to fifty students in every grade, and if you have ten of them off to college every day, where's your class? There's no unifying factor in your class. So, I'm glad it's gone. It was bad. I didn't even learn much in those college classes. Yale isn't even taking the credit. I thought select AP classes were harder than the college classes would ever be. The college classes didn't prepare me, but the AP classes did.

Did the ACT? I get that it is obviously important for our state because the state really emphasizes the benchmark. That one ACT in March of your junior year is the biggest thing that's ever happened to anyone. Yeah, it's like super extra. But the ACT for me, I didn't ever really care that much. I did well on it. It was great for me. I have a thirty-five.

So, the school, they actually always ask me to tutor everyone. Before the March ACT, like a couple months before, I would tutor my entire junior class. And then this year, I also would tutor the new juniors. So I don't know what they're going to do next year when I'm not tutoring everyone. This sounds kind of arrogant, but I would teach better than the teachers would for the ACT. And that's because I've taken it, and I know what I'm doing. Also, a lot of students who wouldn't normally pay attention would pay attention to me because it was their peer as opposed to an adult. I think I'm a lot more approachable. I was like, "Okay, well, this is how we're gonna do it. This is not the way you should learn it. This is not the correct way, but this is the way that will get you a good score." And the teacher, she would always roll her eyes and go, "Oh my god Akhil. Here you go again. This is not the way you should be teaching it."

There is a lot of pushback against the ACT. People say, "Oh, it's not really measuring someone's intelligence." Overall, I feel that intelligent students do better. Obviously, there are exceptions. There are exceptions to any rule, but I think elite colleges tend to see that. I know lots of people who have lower thirties who got in, but their GPAs are still like a 4.0 or a 3.9.

I think with the ACT, yes they're trying to get rid of it, a lot of people are saying that rich people tend to get better scores, but I think they're getting a better education a lot of times, and that's where the income divide then shows up on the ACT. It's nothing to do with them getting more prep because I feel like a lot of times, you can prep all you want, and this is from my experience teaching people, and you're not going to go up more than two points. You're going to have to have gotten some extra education to push your score up or understand it in a different context. For instance, I know my friend, she took the test so many times, and she kept getting the same score. I know she had prepared more, and I know she understood the test more, but it wasn't helping her. But I think it does show a general level of academic ability. There aren't many opportunities in places like eastern Kentucky. The ACT is one of the few ways to actually stand out when you compare yourself to kids who've had opportunities to work with major companies or in research labs, something not possible in places like here.

In terms of college, there's definitely a lack of resources if you're trying to do anything that's not the norm. The last student who went to a top tier university, he went to Harvard, was in 2005. And the last National Merit Scholar was in 2008. Finding scholarships and stuff like that was almost impossible because everyone here was going for scholarships associated with their schools, but the schools I was applying to didn't have those sort of scholarships. Like Yale's not going to give me a scholarship to go there.

If I didn't have the internet, I wouldn't have been able to do anything. Using sites like FastWeb on the internet showed me where to find scholarships and things like that. I think that's the way for rural areas to compete with major cities in terms of representation at elite universities. Right now, rural areas in America are super underrepresented, even with plenty of intelligent people there. They just don't have the connections to apply to those places. They don't understand what it means. They don't understand how to get there, and it seems like a really foreign concept to them.

I think the internet is basically the saving grace for rural communities. From my experience, that's where I would find stuff out, even toxic College Confidential would help me a lot because at least I had articles that were linked on there that I would read that would help me realize what to do to get into those universities.

Living here on the whole is definitely an experience, and when I talk to people outside they're like, "I don't really get it." And I just say that you'll have to come visit or something. I don't know, I don't think I've ever felt, like, "one with Eastern Kentucky." I think I've always kind of felt like an outsider, but I try, in my own philosophy of life, I try to take things I don't like about something and turn it into a way that I learn something.

I'm not going to say that I want to live here after college or that I'm never coming back, but I can respect that I lived here and how it changed my life and how it shaped me. I can't say that, had I lived in New York City, my life would be the same. I think we all have our own circumstances; it's what we make out of them that's important. And some people may have had a better experience. Maybe they went to a college prep school in New England and going to Harvard is easy, but that's their story, and this is mine. I guess it's kind of like a symbol that you can beat the odds or whatever. The odds here are low that you're going to go anywhere else, but every person here has the chance to, if they tried.

My family is from all over the world, so it's not a big deal for me to be like, "I'm moving. Goodbye." I think our state is kind of a problem in that fact. They kind of encourage people to stay in our state, that idea of the whole "brain drain" thing. State loyalty is valued, but I'm like, "If you're getting better opportunities elsewhere, why would you not take them?"

In Eastern Kentucky, the idea of leaving is so foreign, they're like, "But my whole family is here, every single one of them lives up in the holler." My friend's family told her, "You're abandoning us." And that's such a common sense I get here a lot. I've had a couple people ask me, "Why don't you just go to UK (University of Kentucky)?" Like, is this even a question? So I think there's a huge amount of animosity toward people leaving. There's almost a pain from people leaving because they don't come back. People definitely try to make you feel guilty because you're leaving here. They always ask me whether or not I'm leaving forever, and of course I say no. A little white lie never hurt anybody.

There's a level of ignorance. That's such a problem that people from outside are not coming in. There's no Hispanic people. There's no black people. There are no other cultures coming in. I feel like the more you meet people, the less you are to be like that. We had a Hispanic kid in our grade for a day, and then they left. There's a couple of black people in our school. But you can count them. I'm the cultural diversity in my grade. Being half-Indian, everyone's like, "Oh my god, you're so diverse. Diversity!" I think that lack of diversity is a huge problem.

So my admissions officer at Yale was the first Ivy League admissions officer to ever visit the Appalachian region. Ever. She's the Kentucky representative, because there's a representative for almost every state, but she says that every Ivy League officer always goes to Louisville, and then every year, they switch between Lexington and Bowling Green. And those are the only places they'll visit, and then they'll go back. And so, this year, she was new to Yale, and they were like "Okay, you're going to Louisville, but would you rather have Lexington or Bowling Green?" And she said that she wanted to go to Appalachia. They were completely shocked. She was the first person to ever visit our region from any Ivy. Yale was straight up like, "What are you talking about? Why do you want to go there?" And she was like, "Shut up, I'm going." So, I was like, "You're such a rebel."

She said she met someone who had never driven outside of Whitesburg, like the city limits of Whitesburg, ever. But that idea is a common thing; people don't leave. People who are more in poverty can't afford to go to different places and stuff like that, and they don't have the resources to learn about it. You know how they have the cycle of poverty-type idea? It's like a cycle of education. If you don't have someone breaking it, everyone's going to keep following. And I'm not saying I'm the person breaking it, because I don't have younger siblings, I don't have anyone to follow my footsteps, but here, at least, since there are two students going there, I would bet you that next year at least one does. Maybe not Yale, but some place similar. But I think not a single student next year at our school is applying somewhere out of state.

So when I went to LA, I visited my cousin, and all of the people at USC were like, "Where are you from?" And I was like, "I am from Eastern Kentucky, in the mountains." And they were all like, "But how did you apply to USC? I've never met anyone from anywhere in that region." And I was like, "Yeah, probably not." They would always refer to stereotypes. And they would be like, "Do you wear shoes? Do people actually wear shoes?" And I was like, "Yeah, people wear shoes." Everyone from Eastern Kentucky is automatically seen as dumb. Even from Lexington, people think that. I think because the admissions officer came here, it gave me a better chance of getting in.

It's funny though, my admissions officer at U Chicago wanted to meet me. He emailed me and was like, "Please meet me while you're here. We never have students apply from your area. I was just so excited that you applied, and your application was great and everything. It's just super cool that you're actually trying to apply here."

Looking back, the small school had its perks. There is no pressure to be socially at the top. We only have forty people. There's not cliques and stuff. There's like the smart students and the not-as-smart students, the athletic students and the not-as-athletic students, and those all are mixed together. If I went to a larger school, I think I would have been a lot more lost. I don't really fit in with the typical culture here, but there is a community sense that helped me through it. I have lots of friends. Like everyone in our grade is friends. Obviously, we don't get along all the time because that's not how life goes, but we all know each other. And if I saw any of them on the street I would say hi, and we would have a conversation about how life was going. So I think that's something that's really nice about growing up here.

I think other students have that power to make you feel worthwhile as opposed to the administration just ignoring you. I think that school administrations ignore that a lot of times, but fellow students and individual teachers can really make your life so much better. If it weren't for my friends or teachers, I don't think I could've done it. I'm so thankful for the teachers I've had. Yeah, I think that's it.

The Oddsbuckers
Elizabeth

"And now it's my turn to start my story, and I am not about to let any of these difficulties get in my way."

Not many people from around here want to be a biologist, but I do. I've been looking at colleges that offer programs and will let me major in biochemistry and animal studies, and I found some universities in state that are appealing to me. All I want to do is work in a lab or in a hospital, finding solutions to help people. I know that's a really lofty goal, but I've tried to prepare myself the best I know how.

Taking the ACT was a big step in getting there. I took my first go at it sophomore year, and it was two weeks before school would be out for the summer. The funny thing was that I didn't even know I had to take the ACT. A lot of people question why I took it so early in the first place, but I was in honors math classes, so the next math classes I was supposed to take were college-level courses anyway. I realized too late that the registration for the last ACT of the year was coming to a close, and I rushed to talk to my counselor. I was like, "Can you help me?"

And she's like, "Yeah, come by my office, and we'll get it done. You can use my credit card and just pay me back. Sound good?"

I was in total shock. That was more than good, that was absolutely amazing. I couldn't believe what she was offering to do for me, considering the fact that I had never met her then, never even talked to her. She ended up signing me up for it, and I got that taken care of. The next year I took Algebra II and Pre-Calculus the year after that, and now, I'm finished my first year as a college freshman. She is one of the main reasons why I am going to college.

See, the problem is that there's a lot of smart people, but the benchmarks are considered when you're smart enough. There are a lot of people who are intelligent but just can't test. And I hate that. It seems so unfair. What did I do differently than the kids in my honors math classes with higher grades to get a better ACT score?

I think the test can be used to measure college readiness to an extent, but it bothers me when certain kids don't get that benchmark no matter what they do, how much they study, or how hard they try. After taking it several times, I feel like the test is structured in a very narrow and precise fashion. It doesn't allow for creativity, expression, or innovation. It relies on a very strict thought process, and if you don't think in the same way as the test makers, then you're out of luck. And then, on top of that, some of my friends suffer from testing anxiety. I'm so grateful I don't experience that because I have seen so many lives and futures ruined because of it. To put it bluntly, it sucks.

The majority of the people here want to go to college, the key word being "want." There's a lot of kids that are, like, all about college, and they're all about their career and life, but then things get in the way. Like my sister, for example, was going to go to college and do all that, but she fell in love, had a baby and never went. I mean, she's tried to go back, but life kept getting in the way you know? And there are a lot of people who are like that. She is definitely not an extreme.

Money and family. That's what's stopping us. It is so much more than academics. A lot of people don't want to move far away because of their family that been in this county for the last century. A lot of people here are foster kids and don't have any money to go to college. A lot of my classmates don't want to because they never grew up in a family and were never encouraged to achieve their dreams, not by their parents, their friends, their teachers. So they were like, "Why even try?" I know a lot of kids like that—too many kids like that.

A lot of kids' parents are like, "Just do what you want, it doesn't matter." And then the students will be in here, in the classrooms, being rude to teachers. They'll have an F on their midterm and won't think twice about it because they can make it up in credit recovery. Between you and me, recovery is a joke. It's really easy since you do it on a computer and can look up the answers. So what is the point in wasting all our effort in the first place, right? There isn't a lack of knowledge or intelligence in my school, just a lack of hope. No one daydreams anymore.

Everyone knows what the FAFSA is. It's just they don't really care. They don't care, and they don't want to know. School force feeds us all these acronyms—FAFSA, ACT, SAT, PSAT (Preliminary SAT)—and we briefly go over them in class because teachers have to, but no one really knows what's going on, what any of those letters stand for, or that they are the people most eligible to receive all the financial assistance. And so ironically, the people that are actually the ones most likely to get money don't end up going to college for "financial reasons."

When the counselors talk, they always talk about credits in your school. They talk about it so much. It's the same thing over and over and over. They don't stress over anything else apart from, "This is what you've got to do to graduate!" Because of this, I'm pretty sure us seniors are going to graduate with more credits than anybody else in the school, and it's crazy. It becomes so stressful when they talk to you because that's all they talk about. But when you talk about college, they say, "We'll have to look into that" or "We will get back to you later," and they never do.

I have a lot of friends in fast foods who continue to work there even after they have graduated. A lot of them plan on going to factories. A lot of people go to places like the major car manufacturer down the road, and they think, "Oh I'll go earn some money!" But it's just not a steady job. If you don't have the skills they're looking for, or if you haven't been to trade school, you can get laid off the first week, and then, what are you going to depend on? I mean, if you actually have a career, it's something you can rely on for the rest of your life. It makes no sense to me why they have that mindset. They say they'll do it later. They'll save up later, go to college later, get out of the town later. They don't end up achieving anything. Later is just their way of coping with the reality.

My dad went to trade school and studied a lot of welding. My dad doesn't have a degree or anything, but he's worked in factories. He's worked for car manufacturers, infrastructure, built houses. If it requires two hands, anything you name, he's probably done it, and he's good. Right now he's a mechanic for a huge company that is willing to send him to school to learn more about tractors. He's excited, but like the high school students, is hesitant to take the promotion because it would mean that he'd be far away from his family for a few months. He thinks that's too large of an issue.

My mom went to school to be a teacher. She was only two credits shy from graduating when she decided she did not want to go through with it anymore. So then, she decided to go into nursing. She wanted to be an RN (Registered Nurse) and has actually had her CNA (Certified Nursing Assistant) for a long time. She worked in a nursing home before she had my little brother. After his birth, she got hurt, and she couldn't work in a nursing home no more. Then she was going to be a therapist, decided against it again, and ended up quitting, again. She then figured out that her true passion was journalism. She's a great writer, I can promise you that. I've read her poems that she's wrote and published, and they're amazing. I wanted her to give it a shot, for real, so badly, but she's just done with school. She thinks she's too old and tells me that she has to focus on her grandchildren right now.

And now it's my turn to start my story, and I am not about to let any of these difficulties get in my way. I didn't know where I was going or what I was going to do, I didn't have any idea. I kinda had an idea of what I wanted to be and what college I wanted to go to, but other than that, I wasn't really sure about anything else. So when my counselor signed me up for the ACT, I decided to take it. Turned out I passed it, so I was like, *Yeah that's pretty good!* I was four points above benchmarks, so I was pretty psyched about that. I didn't even study because I was at a camp that summer, and I got home, and my mom was like, "You've got two days." I actually sat on the couch for those two days, but I didn't really study. I was so tired. I have no idea how I even got the score I did. Probably just luck, if we are being honest.

I tried to get ahead on my classes, take college courses in high school, so I don't end up like my other family members. I actually tried signing up for a lot of AP classes. I turned in the papers—correction—I was the first person to turn in the papers, to send them in to take the test. And as luck would have it, my counselor lost them, all of them, and she admitted it. So I had to make the payments twice and take the makeup test for those AP exams. I never got to go to the day of the actual test, the day I had already paid for. I was so mad about that because I spent the whole year taking three AP classes, studying for them so hard, only to be told that I not only would be able to not take the test on the day I had planned, but I had to pay extra.

Right now, I think I'd be way better off at college than I would be at high school. I mean I hate being far away from family and want to see them every day, but I can still do it because I enjoy it, the college atmosphere. I won't have counselors constantly breathing down my neck. You can constantly remind yourself, and I like that better.

I'm going to get a degree for one and start a career and get successful in life. I'm going to build relationships with people, like diversity and different groups, you know, and kinda have that stronghold. I'm going to find out as much as I can and use that to find a way to help people more than anything.

The Oddsbuckers
Jule

"For those that do want to go to college, it's just a damper. We are not the same as everyone else. We are the outsiders looking in."

School has made me hate Spanish.

It wasn't always this way. My freshman and sophomore year, we had a teacher that was with the school for at least three decades. She taught the exact same thing each and every year, and she handed out packets that were thirty years old. I always thought that was weird, you know? Like, if I want to learn how to speak Spanish, I want to know how to talk to the people of today, not the people that lived thirty years ago. I literally have friends who are twenty-five and graduated from college that had the same packets. And no, I'm not kidding. It's a small town. People don't really move away.

She didn't really teach the material, and she didn't care because she had her tenure or whatever. She retired my junior year, so we had a Spanish teacher come all the way from Spain to take her place. He was obviously legit because he had taught students all over the world. I was thrilled at the idea that my classes would be engaging, relevant, and actually, like, real. The excitement didn't last though because he ended up teaching the lower level class, and I was in Spanish II. Even worse, it was a one-year deal. That was it. He came and left, just like that. I think that he went back to Spain to teach English. Sounds like a better job anyways. I think he realized that people get stuck in here and left when he had the chance.

Now we take Spanish online. Each student sits there and learns Spanish, not from a teacher, but a computer. Instead, our teacher is now—wait for it—the school's athletic director. He's not even technically a teacher. He just sits there and kinda monitors everybody. It's pathetic, really. There is this lack of incentive, and by that I mean that the teachers don't try to push you at all. I mean, they care about the people that listen, like me. But if the student isn't already convinced that they matter, they don't try to convince them otherwise. The kids that need an attitude change and a shift in perspective never get a second glance.

For the most part, I've been in this little town my whole life. There is no culture, no diversity, nothing. Everybody is exactly the same. We eat the same food, do the same things for fun, know the same people, and we even shop at the same stores. I know exactly where every girl in my school gets their outfits and how much they pay for them. It's the same kind of people, so it is no surprise that the majority of our students want to go into farming. I guess that's fine, to each their own. But for those that do want to go to college, it's just a damper. We are not the same as everyone else. We are the outsiders looking in. Being different isn't only about race or religion anymore.

I just don't think students here are raised in a background that encourages going to college. Even the school doesn't prepare us for it. I look down the street, and I think about all the amazing schools that exist in the bigger parts of Kentucky, just a couple hours down the road. I hear stories about their programs, about their classes, about their teachers, and I just get so jealous. They actually have real human beings teaching their classes. I just wish I could have a part of that. My English teacher makes me feel that way. She's amazing. I mean she's taught me and so many others so much. The rest of our teachers are kinda pathetic. Like, they really are. They don't care. You need to be very prestigious with your work and know what you're talking about if you want to get any attention from them. I can count on one hand the number of students that these teachers truly take into consideration.

The people that I hang out with want to go to college for the most part. I don't like hanging around people who say that they don't want to go to college, because it seems like they don't want to do anything with their lives or have no plans for the future. Even worse, no one seems to care. Everyone acts like it's completely normal. Have you ever watched a horror movie, and you can see the monster hiding behind the main character? The character doesn't know that the monster is there, but everyone watching the movie does, and no matter how much you scream at the screen, you can't change the plot of the movie. That's how I feel. I am screaming and no one around me seems to notice that their futures are being attacked.

I'm very keen for school. I just got accepted into the University of Kentucky, and that's where I'm going. I'm very excited, but I know that I've worked very hard for it. I participate in absolutely everything that the school has to offer. I have been part of the Y-Club, lead the Future Business Leaders of America Club, play a huge role in Beta Club, and even took six AP classes. Six! When I graduate, I'll have nine college credit hours from taking dual credit classes. My boyfriend, well, I guess my fiancée now, proposed to me a few weeks ago. His brother graduated from Transylvania University two years ago, and now he's in law school. Can you believe it? I talked to him a ton, and he's really helped me out a lot.

I talked to my college and career readiness lady, too. I kind of feel bad for her. I feel like she works very hard, but not many people care about what they want to do in the future. They don't feel like they have the option of going anywhere else but the major factory plant down the street. They don't see anything bigger for themselves besides that, and those that do have to do a lot of work on their own to figure everything out. People in the bigger cities join Beta Club and Y-Club like it is no big deal, but here, I have to work so hard to keep the programs going. I do so much work on my own to figure everything out. Opportunities exist, but no one, and I literally mean *no one*, in this county has any idea how to find them or what to do about them.

I need to get out of here—I have to get out of here—but I'm afraid of what everyone will say. What if they think that this place that was good enough for my entire family isn't good enough for me? Like, I have known everyone here since the day I was born. I have been in classes with the same forty people from preschool all the way to senior year. People who aren't from here tell me that they have only heard about this type of life in movies.

Now, here is where the plot of the movie gets messed up. I don't care if it is a horror movie, futuristic movie, or just a romance. This part doesn't add up. Last year, I finished with a 4.0. I got an A in every single one of my classes, including the AP classes. I led all of these clubs, stayed on top of my school work, and studied a lot.

I got a twenty on the ACT.

Can you tell me how in the world that adds up? I personally just do not see how that adds up! I think your GPA shows way more than your ACT score because you can have a horrible headache or terrible test anxiety. Your effort goes into all the coursework that you do. I do not think that the ACT is a good measurement of a student's intelligence. I just cannot get over the fact that I didn't meet benchmarks in some of my classes when I am working day in and day out to get good grades.

I wish I knew a better way to test students—I've thought about it a lot. I get what the ACT is doing. I mean, it's an easy way to standardize and measure somebody's intelligence. But how is this test is supposed to tell me if I'm college ready? I know plenty of people that got outstanding scores on it and didn't even make it through the first few weeks of college. That is not an exaggeration.

I have a friend who has a thirty on the ACT. He didn't have good grades at all. He slept through all of our classes together, and did not invest in his education. He couldn't care less about what he got on the ACT. When he graduated, he went to the University of Kentucky for his first semester. My high school made a huge deal about it and praised him for all of his "hard work." Everyone was so interested in what would happen to him and what amazing things he would accomplish in college.

A few weeks later, he dropped out. And now, he doesn't do anything. Now, everyone here is thinking, "If this guy with a thirty on the ACT can't do it, then I surely can't if I only have a twenty-three." Any possibility of hope was lost for a while. The student that dropped out lives at home back in this county. It's really depressing. The monster always ends up dragging you back, but I'm not going to let it catch me.

The Oddsbuckers
Hiba

"If I didn't have my parents, I honestly don't think I would be in college right now. I would have probably dropped out my first year."

High school is a complicated story. That's when I got sick.

It was right in the middle of high school. When I was fourteen, I got diagnosed with this weird disease that they call Cerebellar Ataxia. I stopped going to school then to focus on my health, and I didn't go back until I was sixteen.

When I was a sophomore, I went to the hospital because I lost my walking. I didn't know why. I was in the hospital for a month. For the rest of the school year, I just did homeschooling and took it easy at home. I was still unable to walk or use my wheelchair. I went back my junior year because I could finally use my wheelchair to get around, and it was awesome. Everyone was so welcoming when I first came back, but in a weird way. I felt like they were being super nice to me, more nice than usual. It made me happy at first, but it made me feel isolated and different.

It was super weird for me just 'cause I could see everyone walking, and I couldn't. They could go by themselves from class to class, and I couldn't. They could go up the steps without thinking twice, and I couldn't.

It completely changed the way I live my life because even right now, as a senior in college, I don't know exactly what caused my illness. I just know that I can't walk or use my fine motor skills, and the use of my right hand is limited. I was right handed, so I had to learn to use my left hand. It made me work harder because I had to figure out how to do things differently. For example, in the morning, a normal person would get out of bed and go to the bathroom. They would do whatever you have to do. It takes like fifteen minutes total. I had to learn to not just get out of bed but put myself on my wheelchair in the morning. Then I have to transfer and do all sorts of things to get ready. What would take you fifteen minutes initially took me upwards of two and a half hours. I had to learn how to manage my time, and it was difficult. I didn't know when I was supposed to start getting ready for things, and it's just something I've picked up with the years.

The transition to college was way different. It was bigger, and also people didn't really know how to handle people with disabilities. They would hold doors for me and stuff—and they still do, and that's nice. They don't know what to say sometimes. Other times, they'll make plans to go somewhere, and they don't think about how it might not be feasible for me.

College was a huge change for me because I had to learn to be even more independent than I was. Honestly, I don't think I could've done it without my friends and family helping me out. Transitioning to the place where teachers didn't tell me to do things I just kind of had to do them, that wasn't too bad. I was already used to that because they trained us in high school, but I needed much more adult support than any of my friends.

I would need my parents to help me with my disability. They would come visit me sometimes, more times than my friends would call or text theirs. It was odd having family in college, but everyone understood. Other than my unique situation, however, I feel like I was pretty well prepared for college.

I'm majoring in education, and so I have one more year because I decided I didn't want to take more than twelve credit hours per semester. Next year, I'll just be student teaching. It'll be like I'm a student, but I'm not really. I always wanted to be a teacher ever since I was a little kid. I used to take my sister up in the guest bedroom and tutor her against her will in math. She hated it, but her grades did improve. I remember thinking, "I really like this!"

Even after I got diagnosed, I still really wanted to be a teacher. I knew that I needed to go to college, so I made sure that I prepared. When I was a junior in high school, I took all advanced classes. My senior year, I took one AP class, and the rest of my classes were still advanced. I feel like that got me ready for college. I also took the ACT once. I didn't feel like taking it more than that, so that's how I prepared academically.

Socially adapting to college was a little bit more tricky, besides my health issues. I went to an all girls high school, and it was mostly full of white people. It was different going into college and interacting with so many diverse groups. It was a really good change of pace, but it was also kinda overwhelming. I was really nervous that I wouldn't fit in. I realize now that's silly, but it was really concerning. A lot of my friends chose to go to the University of Kentucky or Bellarmine, so I was going into college with only one friend. I was scared that I wasn't going to make friends or that people were going to treat me differently because I'm in a wheelchair. After I came to college, I saw how life on campus actually was, and I realized it was really diverse. I felt more secure. I felt like this wasn't bad. I could do this.

Right now I get disability insurance. That's $733 a month, so that only covers my rent, my sorority bill, and food. My parents are helping me out with the tuition, and I'm also getting some scholarships. One is for continued academic success. It's called the Kentucky Educational Excellence Scholarship. There's a minority teaching scholarship here at the University of Louisville, so I get about twenty-five hundred dollars per semester. U of L was actually not my first choice when going to college. I really wanted to go to UK just because a lot of my friends went there. But then my parents suggested I stay in the same city as them just in case anything happens. I'm glad I did that.

Within the first months of being in college, I forgot to pay my bills. I knew that I had to swallow my pride and ask my parents for some money. I was relieved to see that they weren't too upset. It was nice to know that they would always be there for me. If I didn't have my parents, I honestly don't think I would be in college right now. I would have probably dropped out my first year even though I'm academically ready and did well in high school. It's not just money. They support me morally and emotionally. If I do bad on a test or something, they'll talk to me and calm me down. If I need a ride somewhere, they'll give it to me if they're not busy. If they weren't around to help, I feel like I would probably rely on government assistance. I would still try. It would just be a lot harder than it is.

I realized that college is more than just academic achievement. I have my friends, parents, and all this social motivation that I desperately need. I needed someone to fall back on when I couldn't pay my bills. I had to know how to live independently, not just how to do schoolwork. Of course, schoolwork is a big thing. I'm going to be a teacher, and that's awesome, but it's not the only thing that makes me happy. I'm also in a sorority and just hanging out with them and being a part of that makes me really happy. Being a leader at the disability center at U of L, that also makes me so happy. I'm really passionate about that.

You know what else made me happy here? U of L has a lot of resources for disabled people, and I love that. My high school was private, so it was new and up to date with handicap access. But other buildings that I have noticed, even if they're handicap accessible, have narrow hallways that make it difficult. For the most part, U of L is not like that, and I am glad.

So far, I have loved living independently. I know a lot of people are like, "Hey! I'm going to love that," when they are in high school, but I wasn't always like that. I was scared to live on my own. I was used to my parents doing everything for me. I always had help when I needed it, especially when getting used to my new condition in high school.

Now that I am living on my own, I have to wake myself up. I have to make my own food and clean my own dishes. I was so worried, but it ended up not being so hard. I kept thinking that I was going to hurt myself somehow or some way. I couldn't stop imagining that I would do something when I was by myself that would make my disability worse. I was terrified of being immobile and having no one around. I was scared that it was going to be hard, and it was. Now, I love it. It makes me more productive. It makes me feel good to be able to do things I didn't think I would be able to do alone. I kept saying to myself, "This is independence!"

Now that I look back upon my high school years, I would tell myself to not be afraid. I would tell myself to step out of my comfort zone. When I was a senior in high school, I was really afraid to do anything. I was a lot more shy and reserved. I thought that if I tried anything out of the ordinary, everyone would think bad of me or laugh at me. I'd tell her to be herself, do whatever she wanted to do, and everything would be fine.

I've been sick for six and a half years now, but it wasn't until just last year that I accepted this is how things are. Maybe they're not gonna be this way forever, but there's a possibility, and I have to accept that. I have to know that what's gonna happen is gonna happen, and I can't change it by willing it to change. I have to actually try and work hard. That's when I stopped being sad all the time and started working even harder. College has given me an education and a way to love myself again.

The Oddsbuckers
Heather

"The arts program has given me a sense of belonging. I don't come to school anymore because it is the only option in my county and I have no other choice. I come because I have a reason to"

Our principal is such an inspiration. Me personally, when I go to college, I want to go into education and teach and eventually become a principal myself one day. He makes it his duty and his job not only to make sure the school is a safe environment but that each student feels important. He genuinely wants to know each and every student that walks through his school doors. Some students find it strange that their principal pays more attention to them than their parents.

He knows what we go through. He just wants it to be a home and a safe environment for every student in the county—literally. There is only one high school for the entire county here, and none of us have a choice or luxury of choosing between schools. I have some distant friends that are from richer counties that tell me, there, they have two or even three high schools for their county. I wonder what that is like.

My principal, he doesn't play favorites. He's everybody's best friend and just a great guy. Our teachers usually give off the same vibe. They all care. They're all very driven, and I don't think there's one teacher that genuinely wants to see a student fail. They all want their students to succeed, even though most of the time that isn't the case. Each teacher comes with their own, different teaching method, but they're all great teachers in general.

The principal's son was heavily involved in the arts. As the years have gone by, the school has been putting more and more focus on the arts, but sports still get the big, blown-up focus. It is going to be like that wherever you go, I guess. At least that is what it has been like here for as long as I have lived here. I don't quite understand why throwing a ball gets so much attention and using a paintbrush doesn't. I joined choir my freshman year where there were only seven people in the group. I have been able to see that choir grow from seven to thirty-plus people. I've also gotten to see the rebirth of our drama program. Last year we performed a play called *Making It*. It's kinda like *The Breakfast Club* meets *Mean Girls,* and I actually got a supporting role. And we've got to see the drama program explode.

Kids before the new principal didn't have these opportunities. They never got to explore who they were, to take a leap into the arts if sports weren't for them. The arts program has given me a sense of belonging. I don't come to school anymore because it is the only option in my county and I have no other choice. I come because I have a reason to, and it has nothing to do with my grades, academics, or sometimes even wanting an education. I keep up my grades because some of the extracurricular arts needs me to, and that's it. It's not that I'm dumb; I just don't see the point. I start to wonder how many kids like me went to this school before the new principal and arts program. I wonder if the teachers thought they were dumb when they really weren't.

My principal also places a huge emphasis on the ACT. I have taken it twice and I have reached benchmarks in English and reading. Right now, I am trying to make a benchmark in math too. I hate the ACT. I feel like it is too standardized. Certain individuals learn in different ways, test in different ways. Just because teachers teach in different ways don't mean that they don't know what they are talking about, and the same should go for testing. The ACT, I feel, was created for specific people. If you're not good at math then "Oh, too bad." Or if you're a slow reader then,"Oh, too bad for you." Or if you're not really good at grammar then, "Oh too bad for you. You're going to have to make benchmark, or else you're not smart enough to be in college."

But guess what? I took the ACT, not timed, and I got a twenty-eight on my reading. I know the information. I took another practice test timed and the score dropped to a nineteen. It is not a good measurement of what a student is capable of and what a student can accomplish. It's just not accurate.

Your intelligence and work ethic is not determined by a number you see on a computer screen or a piece of paper. If you can't pass the ACT, don't think you can't do it.

You're more than a number that you see, and that goes for anything in life. You can still apply to college like I am.

I have applied to a local online career and technical school. I know one hundred percent that I want to go to college. I want to go to the official state university—University of Kentucky. One of my good friends that I grew up with is a sophomore at UK. I'm pretty sure she's studying political science, but she also got to give a speech at the induction ceremony for UK freshman. She's so amazing, and I'm going to ask her to be my mentor when I get there, or if I get there.

I'm going to get my general studies done and get my GPA up, and then I'll talk to an admissions counselor and get four classes every other semester at the cheaper community college prices. I'll stay at home with my family for my first three years and finish off at UK. I've made all of these plans about this from school and doing a lot of studying by myself. I've been to a few UK preview nights too. I would have never been this organized if it weren't for my career counselor at school. She is absolutely astounding. I would be a mess if it wasn't for her. Like it would be chaos, like nobody would know what's going on. She just does her job and is so good at what she does. She starts with you your freshman year and gets an idea of what you want to do. As that progresses, she helps you with your plan after high school. She makes sure your plan is concrete and you have an idea, so you're not out in the world with nothing to do. She makes sure you're as prepared as possible. I say "as possible" because there are just some things that I don't feel like I can prepare for.

The Oddsbuckers
Kevin

"I can get paid while going to college! This is just unheard of from where I'm from."

I am a fifteen-year-old who has lived in Laurel County all my life. I was born here, raised here. My parents were born here, raised here. Almost my entire family was born here, raised here.

Laurel County isn't huge, but compared to all the other rural counties of Kentucky, it is pretty large. It is so big that we have two whole high schools in the county instead of one. Don't really know of anywhere near here that does that well, maybe except Lexington that has like six. I can't imagine what that's even like. Here, though, we are large, which is why they split the single Laurel County High School into two different schools: North Laurel and South Laurel. It sounds like something straight out of *The Outsiders*, and in a way it is. This leads to a friendly rivalry of North vs. South, which mainly expresses itself through sports. For a long time, this was all that was notable about us. Others outside Laurel County didn't know about the people here, didn't care about our academic education, didn't glance at our huge problems, but they knew about the sports. I guess it is better than nothing, right?

But then things started to change when CFI was introduced to us a few years ago. Those three little letters changed the world for me. The Center for Innovation. It was a state-of-the-art facility where students are actually prepared for careers and college in a unique, effective way. CFI was implemented as a separate high school from both the North and South, but allows attendance from students of both schools. Students go half a day at their "home school" and half at the CFI. It was this bridge between two siblings that knew each other at birth, but were separated over time, and I loved it.

While at the CFI, students attend their math, English, and a technical class. Technical classes include subjects and areas of study that I didn't even know existed: biomedical science to allied health, media arts, and engineering. I thought there were only classes I would be able to take in college when I was supposed to be smarter. I thought these were things I would never be able to learn because I, maybe, wouldn't be able to attend or afford it. Each of these are three-year-long programs. I am in the biomedical science program, which I will be completing upon my graduation in 2019.

The first year of biomedical science, which I finished just recently, was focused on finding the cause of death of a fictional thirty-six-year-old woman, Anna Garcia. We dived into the role of a crime scene investigator, an emergency medical technician, and a coroner, among other professions. We didn't just read about these situations in books anymore. No more meaningless handouts. No students sitting in class on their phones. No arguments. The entire world came to life in our classroom. The things we were learning were real. They were alive.

Not only did this give us the opportunity to earn college credit, it gave us valuable insight into a future career that we would not have had at any other school. Out of any of my past classes, I was never given more preparation for a specific career path than in this past year. I love this field so much, and what troubles me is that I would have never known that this is what I wanted to do until I had this chance. If CFI didn't come to Laurel County, I would have had no idea what I'd end up doing. I'd probably figure it out, but I know I would not love it as much as I love my biomedical class.

Perhaps the greatest asset given to students from the CFI is preparation for a job immediately after high school. This is done by giving the students that complete the three-year program certifications, each differing depending on the program the student completed. When I graduate in 2019, I will have a pharmacy technician certification, which will give me the opportunity to have a good paying job while I attend college. I can get paid while going to college! This is just unheard of from where I'm from.

This level of post-high school readiness in a regular school is sparse, as my "home school" has only put emphasis on either the End-of-Course Exam (EOC) or the ACT.

Every time the ACT is administered at the school, the phrase "college and career readiness" is thrown around. It has gotten to the point where the phrase is now just a platitude more than anything with substance to it. This phase has not only been said so many times that it is meaningless, but also it is contradictory to the way schools are run in Laurel County. When a teacher or principal say that they focus on college and career readiness, I can guarantee you that they are exclusively talking about the former. I tend to be pretty active in school, and I still have absolutely no idea what it means. To be honest, I doubt that I would get anywhere even if I asked the teachers. They seem just as confused as I am most of the time.

To say that my school system prepares us for college is a drastic understatement. While many students have learned how to guess on a test question that they do not know, not a single student has been taught how to do taxes or how to apply for a job. Explain to me how in the world we are supposed to make the jump from living with our parents for our entire lives to being thrown in the chaos that is adulthood. Are we supposed to mature over a small timespan of a few months? Is there something that I am missing here? Do the schools expect all these "life skills" to be taught by parents? I can assure you that not a single student is learning any of them at home. Ask me. Ask any one of us.

This emphasis on college completely ignores practical teachings, which would help every single student no matter their plan for their future. This is the official curriculum, so even teachers that want to teach us things that could actually help us simply can't. They are too preoccupied trying to teach content that has to be covered. Anything else is extra, a luxury.

Despite this, there was one teacher who was dead set on preparing us for our college life as well as our entire adult life. Ms. Mays was my business teacher. While in her class, she usually stuck to the regular teachings that are expected of a business teacher, but it was near the end of the school year that things started to differ. Ms. Mays always said that she was "preparing us for the realities of life." She would print worksheets that showed us how to balance a checkbook, and we even had a week-long project about buying a used car and all the expenses that can be expected with such a major investment.

Ms. Mays was very well-liked within the high school, and she is a shining example of how educators can integrate lessons that will help them prepare for their future with their everyday lesson plans. The bad part of this story is that she was technically breaking school policy. While she was teaching us things arguably more valuable than we have ever learned in the past, she was simultaneously risking disciplinary action.

With such a major contrast from the teachings of the CFI, which as I stated prepares us for an actual career, it remains a mystery to me how schools still place no value in practicality. For the school system to truly prepare their students for their future, it must learn from places like the CFI. The term "the future of education" is used quite often, but I think that the CFI is a unique institution where that term can be applied accurately.

The Oddsbuckers
Danielle

"I know that a lot of people don't like the idea of a community college, and to that all I have to say is there's nothing to be ashamed of—at all."

I am currently a freshman at the local community college.

I am at the satellite campus right now, but pretty soon I'll be transferring to the main campus. So far, college is better than I expected it to be. I was really scared of going to college. At first, I had planned to go to some really large universities like Eastern Kentucky University or Campbellsville. My mom convinced me that maybe I don't need to go so far away because I was so scared about it. I ended up going to the community college, and it's actually really nice.

I was really scared about the price honestly. My mom is a single mother, and we're living with my grandparents right now. So it's kind of rough for us to get the money situation under control. She makes a little over ten dollars an hour being a pharmacy tech. So I applied to EKU and Campbellsville, and I got the acceptance letters with the bills in them. EKU said twenty-five thousand dollars, and I was like, "Oh my god!" I had no idea it would cost so much. I thought maybe it costs like fifteen thousand dollars—somewhere in there. But it was twenty-five thousand dollars. I just sat there and looked at the letter for a second, and I was scared out of my mind. I was, like, how am I going to afford this?

I was surprised because that is what my teachers had been telling me. Because some teachers in high school will tell you that it will be like ten thousand dollars or fifteen thousand dollars, and other teachers say it's going to be one hundred thousand dollars and that you're going to have loans for life. I thought maybe I should go in the median somewhere. I guess things have changed since they were in college.

I decided to apply for the FAFSA just in case, and I'm really glad that I did. I got my FAFSA, and when I saw the numbers, it was great. My mom convinced me to apply to the local community college just in case too, which I'm glad I agreed to. With me going there, the state was kind enough to give me a little extra because I am the daughter of a single mother. So I'm actually going home with about two thousand dollars in my pocket per semester. They pay for the rest of it—my books, tuition, and everything else.

Most of those things I had to figure out on my own. The counselors and teachers at my high school didn't play a large role in that. A lot of the scholarships that they talked about were like the Governor's Scholars Program and scholarships for kids that were in advanced classes. In my senior year, I didn't take advanced classes because I was burnt out on them. And there were all of these different things for kids in advanced math programs or advanced whatever programs. I was like, *I'm going to scour out whatever scholarships I can,* but I ended up not getting any except my KEES money and FAFSA.

Before senior year, I did take advanced classes, and they stressed me out. It was something awful. I mean, I would break down often. Sometimes in class. My senior year, I decided that I wanted to focus on getting into college and not AP classes. Honestly, they haven't really done me any good so far. I took AP English, AP European History, and AP US History, but they are not at all similar to my college classes.

They were preparing us for the AP exam, whereas my classes are preparing us for things we're going to have to do in our jobs. My English professor actually holds conferences for every paper that we write. She lets us come into her office, ask her questions, she helps out and puts us on the right train of thought. Then she gives it back to you and you can fix it and get a good grade. So it's not like you're going to be on your own and no one is going to help you with this paper. She's very kind and wants us to get good grades. I haven't had a history class yet, but the way he taught was similar to how my professors teach. Just talking, take down the notes, and there you go. But for the most part, my college classes aren't like what my AP classes were like at all.

I'm doing fine in college now, and it was not because of the classes I took. Probably how hard I worked combined with my ACT score. I'm going to be in the priority bunch that are going into the physical therapy assistant program. So as long as my grades are up, and my ACT score has already set me up to be in that position, I'm going to be accepted as soon as I apply. I got a twenty-four on the test, which I am really excited about, and I only had to take it once. Even with that score, I don't think the ACT was a good representation of how well I would do in college. I'm actually really decent in science, but I got below the benchmark in science on the ACT. I'm in a science major right now, and I got all A's and B's, so I don't think it was very accurate.

My family has lived here all our lives. I was born and raised in Kentucky; a lot of my friends are the same way as well. We all started out wanting to go to college, but then they drifted. I didn't want them in my life anymore because they were kinda "eh," and they weren't focused on their education anymore. Some went to college. I know that some have already dropped out of college, the ones that went to bigger universities. Out of my entire friend group of about fifteen people, I only know one other person who is still in college.

My mom was the one that really pushed me to college. She made a lot of mistakes. When my uncle died, that was her younger brother, she grieved very bad. That's probably not the right word. But she dropped out of college for being a radiologist and she went back and forth and back and forth and she ended up being a physical therapy tech. Now she is a pharmacy tech, and she's not making very much money anymore. So she's not wanting me to make those same mistakes that she made, and she's pushing me to go to college and get a job. I may even go back and be a physical therapist, I'm not sure yet. But she doesn't want me to drop out and make the same mistakes that she made.

I'm living with my family right now, because the college doesn't have dorms or apartments for students to rent out. It's close enough for you to commute. That's why there's a north and south campus, and there are campuses in other counties, but the main campus is about forty-five minutes away. So when I do, I will have to commute, but it won't be that far.

Right now, my college lets me focus on the field of study that I am going into. There are a lot of things that I learned that I probably won't need. I probably won't need a lot of the things that I learned in AP English. I probably won't need anything that I learned in history. I think more clear guidelines on career pathways in school would be helpful.

My school had them, but they didn't offer a lot of help to the kids that were completely clueless on what they were going to go into. This would have helped me, especially now with my classes. Students who have no idea what they want to study are those that need career pathways the most.

I was undecided for a little bit. I went to my mother for help because she, of all people, could help me with something. But there were kids who had no idea what they wanted to do and their teachers were telling them, "You need to figure it out. You need to figure it out," and pressuring them and scaring them. They tell people that I'm in classes with right now that they don't need to have a major picked. They can talk to counselors, they can take inventories, but they don't have to be decided right now.

They also pressured you about how hard college would be, but I was shocked, actually. My anatomy professor straight up told us that if you don't do the work, you're not going to pass. I was like, "Okay, they're not going to wait for every kid to get the work in before they move on." I'm not saying that it's a bad thing, but it confused me because I was used to being so far ahead of the class, and the way they do it in college is either you do it or you don't do it. And if you don't like it, you figure out, *Hey, maybe this isn't for me*, and go and take another class.

Teachers were always scaring me because they were like, "Your professors are going to want this on the due date, and they're going to get onto you if you don't do it, and it's going to be the end of the world if you don't get that project in." My professors are actually just, "If you do it, you do it, and if you don't, you don't, and that's fine, just make it up some other way." They give out extra credit assignments, and they're really nice and relaxed. You don't have to worry about standing out because every single student is different. Every deadline is a soft deadline if you try hard enough. I know that there are students in my anatomy class who are parents, there are some who are going back to college to progress in their career field, like they're getting paid to go back. There's just so many different people, and you don't have to worry about, *Oh, I'm so different*. It's really not that bad.

I don't know how to explain my future plans. It molds together I guess, because in the process of finishing my Associate's, I'm starting my physical therapy assistant certificate. They'll mix them together so you can get both of them done, and that's what I'm going to do because I'm trying to get done with school as soon as possible.

For any high school student right now, I would say try to focus on those things that you love. Because once you get to college and they start telling you to go to counselors and take these inventories and all of that, it will kind've help you to lean toward those things that you really want to do. So don't let high school kind of crush those things. I used to love to draw, but I gave it up because my teachers were like, "You're not going to make any money that way, and you need to stop doodling on your papers." So I completely quit, and I regret it because I did consider going into graphic design. But I'm happy with what I'm doing now because I want to help people. So if I can't help them through cartoons, I'm going to help them through recovery.

I know that a lot of people don't like the idea of a community college, and to that all I have to say is there's nothing to be ashamed of—at all. It is just as good as going to a four-year, major university. It's just smaller and more affordable, and you don't have to worry about meal plans or housing or anything like that. It's just—you can live with your family, which might not be the best thing, it might be a little bit annoying, but if you can get through it, it's fine. The stigma of going to a community college is something that I just don't understand because it is just as good, if not better. You don't have to spend as much money, you might even get money like me and put it in your savings because the state will overpay you. I love it.

The Oddsbuckers
Grissom Scholars

"Being a first-generation college student is challenging. But I challenge myself to break the mold or the stigmas."

First-generation college students—who in 2012 comprised thirty-three percent of college students—must overcome countless obstacles to achieve what some take as a given.* Yet for these students, the challenges are far from over after reaching campus. Being a first-generation student is one of the most oft-cited predictors of failure to persist to a higher education degree. In six years, only forty percent of first generation students are likely to earn a degree or certificate, compared to fifty-five percent for their second or third-generation peers.†

The Student Voice Team spoke with six members of the Grissom Scholars Program at Centre College in Danville. Each year, ten outstanding first-generation college students receive full-tuition scholarships and additional support services as part of the program, including mentors who support them to succeed at Centre and beyond.

These first-generation students underscore that getting to college isn't the same as getting through it.

. . .

Student Voice Team: In a word, what is it like to be a first-generation student at Centre?

Leah: I think appreciative. Specifically being a Grissom, I do feel like I have support. I feel like I've gotten that from faculty and staff outside of Grissom as well.

Mariama: Community. Being first-generation, it's not something that's plastered on your face—so knowing someone else who's first-gen is something I really appreciate.

Digna: I'm gonna say pioneer simply because I feel like we're paving the way for either our younger siblings or our children if we choose to have them.

Emmely: Being a first-generation college student is challenging, but, in the sense that… I like challenge myself to break the mold or the stigmas that may be associated with being a first-generation student, so it motivates me to do my best.

Drew: I would say adaptive, because you have to be able to adapt to the new situations since it's a new place for all of us, and you just have to be able to go with the flow sometimes and take the challenges as they come.

SVT: Who is your favorite teacher and why?

Leah: I'm really bad at picking my favorite professor or teacher ever, but definitely right now I'm taking a class with Dr. Axtell and it's the hardest class I've taken, but it's a freakin' 110-level class. But he's really good, and you can tell he is a good person and that he actually cares and wants you to become a better student. And he's very cognizant of the fact even though you're at Centre, everybody comes from different backgrounds. He actively engages the differences within individuals to enrich the class conversations.

Emmely: My favorite teacher was my seventh grade teacher. She was my favorite because she was the director of the AVID (Advancement Via Individual Determination) program in my middle school. It was an interview process to get into, and I was constantly missing the interviews because I was late or I'd forget about it, but she continually gave me a chance again and again and again and again. When I finally got to the interview, I was like, "Why did you give me so many chances?" And she said, "Because I see potential in you to go to college, and I know that your parents haven't, so I want to make sure I'm able to help you with that." So she was the first person to believe in me going to college after high school, and that was the first time that I believed in myself as well.

Chase: I would say my favorite teacher was my eighth grade Spanish teacher because eighth grade was a pretty tough year for me, and she was always there. She knew everything about my life and talked to my parents constantly. She was really good at telling when I was having a bad day. She was really my second mom. I haven't talked to her in awhile — I need to text her, or call her, or email her or something.

Digna: I think it also made teachers special when they cared for you outside of the academic realm, when they cared about you in your personal life.

Mariama: My twelfth grade AP Lit teacher. She was really helpful. She would sometimes drive me home after school if I had to stay after for something. She would ask about life at school and things like that, trying to connect those things. She was also really helpful when it came to college. She was one of the ones who brought us to Centre to show us around the school, and even last year or this year, if I needed a recommendation, I would shoot her an email or text her, and she would send me recommendations that I need. She has been really helpful this past year.

SVT: How have your teachers and professors assisted you in navigating the difficult terrain of being a first-generation student? At times, have they at all?

Digna: Unfortunately for me, I didn't acknowledge that I was a first-generation student because it was so normal in my community. So when I was applying for the Grissom Scholarship, and I had to be a first-generation college student, it was the first time I was recognizing why, for lack of better phrasing, I was having such a difficult time in the college process. I think coming to Centre and having the support group I have made me more resourceful and made me acknowledge the additional steps I need to take to find that network.

Leah: I didn't know until my senior year of high school when I went into my guidance counselor's office one day when she said "You have this GPA. Why aren't you taking any AP classes?" And I said, "If I want to go to college, don't I need a high GPA?" And she, who had three hundred other students, said, "How did this slip through the cracks? You're a senior." From that point, while my situation was unfortunate, I was more cognizant to ask those questions and be more inquisitive about things. I know that I may not quite know the right way to do things.

Emmely: For me, in high school, I think the majority of help that I got was from the AVID program and then the people I hung out with. If it weren't for the people I hung out with, I would not have known to take any AP classes in high school or wouldn't have gone down the same path they did. So like my friends were mainly the ones who directed me, but now in college, it's more so the professors. Because now, students here feel like we're on the same playing field although some people do have advantages. Professors for sure nowadays are the ones helping me out.

SVT: Do you think a relationship with a teacher is more powerful for students who are first-generation compared to those that are not?

Leah: Absolutely, from my experience. Last Spring, I took Intro to Econ with Dr. Fabritius at 8:00 a.m., and first thing he asked was, "Who's taken an econ class before?" and only two people didn't raise their hands. But he was first-gen, and I was struggling at the beginning because I had a tougher course load, and I didn't know how to study for econ. It's different. Literally every Tuesday and Thursday I was going to his office at seven in the morning, and not even with questions. We even talked about career paths and different things, but he connected with me. He knew that I was a Grissom and was like, "I know being a first-gen student at a school like Centre is different. I know that you as an individual probably have bigger hurdles than that, but I'm gonna help you in whatever ways I can." And that was being there at seven in the morning, before every Tuesday and Thursday class. He did that because he cared, not because I was a first-generation student. But that connection we had was beneficial for both of us.

Drew: I would say that relationship is really powerful here, specifically because at Centre, it's easier to find that connection. Around here, if you take advantage of it, it can be a powerful thing.

SVT: How do your professors shape your experience at Centre? How do they guide you?

Emmely: We got a list from the Grissom program last year of all the staff and faculty that are first-gen. I noticed that one of the names on there was the advisor for pre-physical therapy, and I plan on going on that route. When I went to her office for advising in the spring, I somehow threw in there that I was Grissom, and she was like, "You're first-gen? Oh my god, me too!" And I was like, "Oh my god, you are?" (I totally knew that already.) So, I've built a relationship with her that's been really beneficial for me. I'm on her radar when it comes to opportunities and applying to grad school. She took me under her wing.

Mariama: I think when professors know you're Grissom or something, they'll hold you accountable. They will look out for you but also hold you accountable to a high standard. First semester, I was in class with another Grissom, and her professor was like, "I know you!" And from that day on, I was always on time, and I did my best.

SVT: Is there anything else we haven't talked about that you want to add?

Chase: To speak on the student-teacher relationship, I have a pretty good relationship with my academic advisor, Kyle, and it's really just built off of just keeping it real and not being more than what you are. It's not forced. We just talk. That's how you build relationships. When we had our orientation thing at the very beginning of the year, we went to his house and had a movie night with him, his wife, and kids. Now, we try to do it as much as we can, watch classic movies like *The Breakfast Club* and stuff. Just being normal. Acting like you're a human being.

Mariama: Thinking about student-teacher relationships, we have a person who's not a professor: Sarah. She really cares—she'll go above and beyond to make sure you have all of the information. Having that as first-gen makes you realize it's okay to ask questions, and it's okay not to know something.

Part Seven
The Village

"It takes a village to raise a child," the old proverb says. And getting a child to college takes just that—everyone.

The Village is the families, the educators, the counselors, the youth workers, and the other community members within and beyond our schools—everybody who comprise the potential support system in a student's life.

The Village is the external force that reflects or rejects what students think about themselves and their prospects for college and life well beyond it.

At its best, the Village reminds students that college is a crucial and collective venture; one that they do not have to navigate alone.

The Counselor
Neomia

"There's this myth that everyone wants to escape Eastern Kentucky, that everybody wants to get out and never go back. For a lot of students, that's not true."

I had always been pretty academically inclined as a student, and I had watched my brothers and my sister attempt to go to college and not finish. And so, early on, I didn't know what college was going to do for me.

In Knott County, there were six of us African-Americans in grade school, and we were all family. I had cousins, and I have two sisters and a brother. My sister had actually gone to the University of Kentucky and returned after a year. It was just so difficult on her financially, socially. She had a hard time fitting in and finding her place. Then my brother, he went to Alice Lloyd College for a couple of years, and he struggled there. He dropped out and enlisted in the military.

When I was in eighth grade though, a lot of things happened in my life. I joined speech and debate in my middle school, and I won a state championship that year. Then I lost a lot of weight because I had always been overweight as a child. I was getting more confident. And then one day, we were sitting at the school, and this guy came in from UK, and he started talking about this brand new program called Robinson Scholars.

It was important what he was saying, but for me, it was even more important who he was because he was an African-American male. I had never seen in my school system, or anywhere around me, an African-American male who had obtained a bachelor's degree or a degree of any type. Instantly, I was attracted to that because of what he represented for me and the possibility.

My family's been in Knott County forever. The area where we lived was actually land that was granted to some slaves following the Civil War and the emancipation of slaves. It was granted to my ancestors, and so we stayed there and worked the land. And that's where my family stayed and lived. I've always been surrounded by family and by friends and had a large extended family growing up.

In Knott, the African-American community is pretty tiny. There's about four different families, so a total of about twenty-five to thirty African-American students. In some ways, the racial dynamic has changed, and in some ways not. I wouldn't necessarily say it's acceptable now, but it's tolerable now. It's one of those things where growing up, you have to acclimate to your environment. You have to learn to be a little bit of a chameleon.

I can't say anybody that I knew was rich. You had your families that were better off, that had more say-so in the school system, that had more say-so within the community. You have your students who come from the "bad" families, and everybody knows who they are and what they do. Growing up, I didn't think we were super poor, but that was relative to what everyone else had around us. Being an adult now and looking back on that, we were pretty poor!

My mother got married at sixteen, and she did not have a high school diploma, and so she went back and she got her GED (General Education Degree). And she worked a job making $3.50 an hour all the way while I was growing up. My father, he had what was considered a good job. He worked for the power company. So that was our income. They were raising four kids on basically his salary. So we had enough to have a home and to always be fed and to always be clothed, but it was financially a struggle growing up.

When I went to Knott County High School, it was two floors, in the shape of an H with a huge gym attached—you know how Eastern Kentucky schools usually have their big gyms. It was not very racially diverse. All of the staff were white, mainly female. I would say we had about 150 to 200 people in my class. Everyone knows everyone's business, where they're going and what they're doing. And everybody's parents know. It was close-knit. It was very segregated in terms of what groups you hung out with, and there were very clear labels of who was with who. It was very rigid, politically and socially.

In high school, I didn't experience a lot of racism. My brother did. It was very difficult for him. But mine was more in middle grades. There was my cousin Josh, my cousin Becky, and Kenya. We were all in the same class together, and my cousin Josh and I got in a fight. The teacher came up to us and said, "That's the problem. We can't put any of you niggers in a classroom together."

Absolutely, she said that!

And it was a huge issue. My mother came in. So did the NAACP (National Association for the Advancement of Colored People). The teacher wasn't fired. She wasn't reprimanded or any of that. She still taught. She taught one of my younger cousins, and she told her that she couldn't go outside and play at recess because she was "too dark already."

At the same time I had teachers like her, I had others that challenged me, made me think, and were very accepting and did a lot of things that brought about cultural awareness. We never learned about black history in school. That wasn't taught to us. I had one teacher who taught about those kinds of things and who brought individuals from different cultures in to speak with us. But other than that—high school, middle school—it was a missing part of history for me.

So I was in high school. I was doing speech and debate, and I had applied to Robinson at UK and gotten accepted. It was a pretty big deal because it was the first time that it had been done. I went to my first summer camp, and I met incredible people. I loved the camp, but I loved the people that I met. I actually met my husband at that first summer camp and some of the people who are still my best friends to this day.

There was the high school component, and then there was the college component. So the high school component was we'd have periodic meetings. People would come visit us at school. They'd check in on us. They were grooming us to be ready. During the summer, we would be with other Robinson Scholars and visit college campuses and just get acclimated to being a college student and also do some career readiness, ACT workshops, that kind of thing to get us ready, to be accepted, to be a member of the community.

We stayed at UK for three weeks, and it was then that I discovered, *Hey, this is a real place. This is somewhere where I can learn and feel comfortable. This is somewhere where I can get educated.*

At Robinson, I got a community. Despite the many things UK offers to students, you still, when you come to UK, have to have internal drive because it is a big university. So you, yourself, have to be able to ask for help, to seek opportunities. I don't believe without having that community of people surrounding me that I would have been able to do that.

I came to UK with a group of people that I already knew, that I was already comfortable with. I was able to have a sound foundation, a platform that I could move out from. I definitely would have gotten myself in a world of trouble if I hadn't had that family that supported me.

When we got to campus, at that time, there were two dedicated individuals who worked with us and worked with our secondary advisors, and we met with them a lot. We would have monthly meetings with them, and then we would have small group meetings every other month where we would come together and discuss issues we were having. So they were just a check point to make sure we were doing okay, to see what we were doing. I still talk to the director to this day, periodically. They were our parents while we were on campus! They weren't invasive, but at the same time, they wanted to make sure we were doing what we needed to do.

For me, coming to UK was exciting. For me, it was a chance for freedom and to push myself. I came in with a perspective as I had spent time on the campus before. So it was somewhere that felt comfortable to me, and there were people there that I knew.

Now, when I got to campus, being on a real campus, not just for the summer, it was very different. Even though I had my group of friends with me, I still sometimes felt a little bit isolated. There was this sense of me always being inferior; I always felt inferior on campus. And partly, it was because I spoke with an accent.

Teachers made comments about it. If I said anything that seemed relatively intelligent, they seemed shocked. That's not something I faced alone. I faced adversity because I was African-American, but more so, I acutely felt that I was Appalachian.

It's not necessarily acceptable to make fun of someone because of their skin color or their ethnicity, but I feel like with my being Appalachian, it's open season. It's just a culture really of feeling other. I didn't just feel other by individuals who were white on campus or those who were more educated than I was or from different places, but by the African-American community. I didn't come from their background. I didn't speak like them, but I also wasn't white. It was just a really awkward place to be, and the only place that I did feel comfortable was with those people that I knew and that understood me and understood the culture that I came from. We would have those conversations together about these different issues that we were facing.

One of my best friends was Affrilachian (African-American and Appalachian). She was there at the same time as I was. She and I are still very close friends. But she experienced the same thing. It was probably the most challenging thing in my life. To go from a point where I felt that I was at the absolute top of my game—I excelled in my academics, did well in my activities, and had a scholarship to what I considered the best university in the state—and then to come here and to feel absolutely like I was at the bottom of the totem pole, like I was not of value here.

Robinson became my refuge. It was where my friends were. I could speak freely. It's where people understood what I had to say and how I was saying it because they were having the same experiences that I was.

Now I work in college counseling. I know from my work as a counselor that Lexington is such a different environment for our students. First, they go home for that comfort of family, the comfort of the environment. And a lot of students come from circumstances in which their families rely on them. For health care for elderly family members, for brothers and sisters, and they may have a farm that they have to help their parents work, and so they have to go home. Their parents, having not experienced college themselves, don't understand that college is a seven-day-a-week kind of endeavor. They're used to an environment where school goes from Monday to Friday, and your weekends are free for family and friends or for your extracurriculars. So their understanding is: "Okay, you're done with class. You can come home and be with us now."

There's this myth that everyone wants to escape Eastern Kentucky, that everybody wants to get out and never go back. For a lot of students, that's not true. They want to be able to get an education and take it back. Home is something that's very important to us. It's embedded. It's a place that we love. Our family structures are so strong that homesickness is a real issue for our students.

I believe there's a financial component, there's an academic readiness component, and then there's also a socially-ready component that goes with it. They all have to be paid equal attention to. Sometimes, there's only a focus on those students who get thirty-ones on their ACT, that sometimes those students who are getting a twenty are really ignored. And a certain aspect of those thirty-one students are ignored. In my experience, the high-achieving students that come in are students that I, as an advisor, have had the absolute most difficulty with. Because they're academically competent, but at the same time, they're not socially competent.

In college, it's about navigating your social world as well as your academic world. For those students, they come in thinking they're ready. But some of those students in high school were not really challenged and so, they approach college the same way they did high school. They don't know how to study. They don't know how to manage their time because they've usually had a parent who has managed everything for them. And so, they fall behind. The students that I see be successful in college are typically those who score a twenty-two or twenty-three on the ACT, who know that they have to work a little bit, who have learned to manage themselves throughout the time they were in high school. You can just sort of let them go and let them do what they need to do with the social support.

Academics in college are important, but we've focused too much on academics. In order for students to succeed, we have to remember that they are individuals. They have different personal issues and things that they come to college with and things that they bring to the table.

The average ACT score of our students is a twenty-five and the range is from a thirty down to a nineteen. All of those students are doing well. They just needed somebody to believe in them and support them, to counter those other things that are going on.

These are the kids that are moving the numbers.

You can't change the outlook of Kentucky, and you can't change the economic reality of Kentucky unless every student is being touched. At this point in time, especially in the Appalachian region, every student that is not being supported academically and socially, that's another student that's going to become a statistic. If we want a better Commonwealth, we really need to invest in every child.

My official position now is program coordinator for Robinson Scholars. We have about three hundred students in the high school program in twenty-nine Eastern Kentucky counties, and then we have about 120 students on the UK college campus.

I also work as the speech and debate coach at Dunbar High School. I did speech all through high school. After I graduated college, I did nanny for a little while and realized that I did graduate college, so maybe I need to do something different than be a nanny. It was a great experience and all, but I wanted to be a little more impactful.

The Teacher
Ms. Paceley

"I am currently a science teacher. I got a nineteen on the science test. So no, the ACT does not measure aptitude, potential, or success."

I teach everything. If you want any student in the entire school to be educated in biology, I am the go-to woman. I teach classes from general freshman in integrated science, to the accelerated program's sophomores, to the juniors in AP Biology. Every single level in this science, I have covered. With these different subjects, you need to have different sets of standards. General is the state standards, and AP is dictated by the College Board, so the standards lend themselves to different levels, just based on these requirements alone. When I go from general to the gifted and talented sections, everything has the same set of standards, but I have to figure out how to teach them at different levels, and it's a struggle. You have to get to know your kids first, before you really know what level they're on, and then you can differentiate your instruction.

Once I get to know the students personally, and sometimes I look at their test scores and reading ability, I deliver material in different ways to see how the students respond best. It might be with a PowerPoint, guided notes, or sometimes I can just say, "Read these textbook chapters. We're going to use this material next class." It really just depends on the kind of students I have. For example, with the gifted and talented group, I can say, "Review this material at home; we are going to apply that knowledge in a lab tomorrow." With the general class, they're most likely not going to do homework or not be able to do homework because of what their outside-of-school lives might entail. So then, all of the learning is in that ninety minutes. There's nothing that's going to happen outside of that class, which just means you just have to be really intentional about what you do pick for them to learn.

All my teaching career has been exam-based. For six years I've been teaching towards the EOC test. In the back of my head, I keep telling myself that I am teaching so that students learn biology, and I am simply relating it to what is on the test. The root of the class is passion and curiosity. But I'm held to this testing standard and compared to everyone else year by year, and the whole science department is looking towards the biology classes for their accountability scores.

In the end, the goal for each individual differs in high school. I think for some people, it's college, but I don't think that's everyone's purpose for high school. I think it's preparing them for life as an adult, if you had to pick one purpose. And that might be pursuing higher education, or it might be pursuing a career, or it might be becoming a parent. Regardless of what it actually looks like for everybody, they have to be an adult in our country. To get to that goal, everyone needs to have responsibility and be able to solve problems. We say in class that deadlines are important and that you never get second chances in your real life, but you do. And deadlines can be pushed in a lot of things in your real life.

Only some of my students are ready for life after high school. Not everybody, but there's only so much you can teach. They're not going to learn until they're there like applying for a job. You can help prepare them mentally and encourage them to study for the test, but you're not going to know if you're prepared until you're in the moment. So unless we have mock adult days, I don't know that we'd actually get them really prepared. But maybe a better sense of what resources are there for them when they fall short of being prepared would be better.

What is most definitely not the way of evaluating readiness for college though is the ACT. When I was in high school, twelve or thirteen years ago, I took the ACT myself, and it in no way told me how prepared I was for college.

I am currently a science teacher.

I got a nineteen on the science test.

I went to college for free.

I have a master's degree, and I'm going back to school to get my second master's degree.

I have a full-time job with job security, retirement.

I can take vacations and still get paid.

I got a nineteen on the science test.

So no, the ACT does not measure aptitude, potential, or success.

What would instead? I think it's a combination. I mean, I also had a 4.0, did extracurricular activities in high school, and was well-rounded. The ACT was only a piece of the puzzle, which I understand, but it didn't dictate everything about whether or not I'd be prepared in the way public policy is currently doing now.

The Teacher
Ms. Henly

"On a systemic level, we really need to stop testing every child the same way."

I had a student that I will never forget a few years ago. She wasn't a refugee, but she was an immigrant. She came here to live with her aunt and uncle, legally. Legally and on a learning visa, I believe. She's from Cambodia, and her parents were still in Cambodia. She told me that she misses them very much, and I remember just not being able to respond to such a situation. I admired her for going all these lengths for her education. There was a certain respect for her audacity, for her risk.

She had a very limited English proficiency, but because of the way the English as a Second Language program works, you really don't have to have that good of an English proficiency to get out of ESL-only classes and come into the general classroom setting. So despite her very limited English proficiency, she had been integrated into my general English classroom setting and was expected to perform at the same level as all of my native English speakers.

According to how our standardized testing situation is set up in the United States, we test everybody the same. The philosophy is a good one, ideologically. Everybody has the same capability of learning. We need to push everyone and hold everyone to the same standards, so we're going to test everyone the exact same. The downside of that philosophy is when the true equity and equality of the situation is measured, does every student really have the same chance? See, the idea of equity is that everyone gets the same thing. This is what we are doing right now by designing our testing system to be as uniform as possible. But really, we should be looking at equality, which is giving everyone what they need individually to succeed. This story really drove that home for me as a teacher. This is what made me change my mind:

It was my first year of teaching with her. Luckily I had known her from my student teaching. She had been in my student-teaching classroom the year prior, and she got to move up with me when I was hired here after that. That was really special; we had already formed a good relationship. So we worked really closely together from the get go, her senior year, and she was one of the most motivated students I've ever had.

It was clear to me that she wanted to succeed here, in the United States, and contribute to our community, make herself better, and support her family back in Cambodia. One of my favorite things about her is that she was grateful for the opportunity her aunt and uncle gave to her. She would always mention wanting to be successful so that she could repay them, in some way, later. I just thought that was really incredible about her. The way that manifested is that she was just constantly wanting extra help. She wanted to stay after school with me. She tried to take every single opportunity that I gave her.

As a teacher, I was working extra hours to try to help her. Her biggest struggle was the ACT. Her math score, I think, was in the upper twenties, maybe even thirties. Clearly this girl had some incredible academic ability. Her English score was a ten or eight. I mean it was really, really low because she was not a native English speaker. And we did everything that we could that year: she stayed after, we did practice tests, special lessons. I would use her own writing from class, and we would go back through to work on grammar rules. I would try to relate that to the test. I told her things like, "You'll see this rule on the ACT. It's been on there in the past, so we need to remember this one." What was remarkable was that I saw her improving in my class. She was performing better on tests, and her classwork was so much better than where she started. But she still wasn't improving on the ACT, which is funny because that test is supposed to reflect academic knowledge. If they're growing in the classroom, they should also, theoretically, if it's a good test, be growing on the test too.

It wasn't just grades either. The good thing about having the school's block schedule is that I get to see my students throughout the entire year. What I noticed specifically about her was her writing ability. Writing to me is one of the biggest reflections of a student's ability to succeed in college. Writing and reading. I was observing her in-class writing abilities and her interpretive abilities. She wouldn't sit in the corner with a look of utter confusion. She began reading passages aloud to the class. She was leading discussions.

But her ACT scores were completely stagnant in English and reading. So I couldn't figure out why that was. I didn't understand at the time because I hadn't done a whole lot of research on the ACT. Now that I have, I do understand.

I look back on this moment that I'm about to tell you about again, and I completely get it. She had stayed after school that day. The December exam, the seniors' last chance to get the score they want, was approaching. She needed to be accepted into college without having to do a bunch of remedial courses. It costs money, and of course, as an immigrant, she didn't have money. She was low income, barely feeding herself, and in no condition to spend hundreds and hundreds of extra dollars on taking the remedial classes in college. From what I saw, she didn't need to. She had the work ethic. She would have figured out how to succeed without the remedial classes just like she was succeeding tremendously in my own class.

We were staying after school on a regular basis, and one day, I was trying to build her confidence. I went into this day thinking, *I've found the easiest passage I could find.* I spent an hour and a half looking through all my ACT prep books that I had gathered, and I tried to find the easiest one with the easiest questions. I wanted her to think to herself, "Oh, you can do this! Look at all you've learned." Once she saw a good score on one passage, maybe that would ease her anxiety, which has also been shown to have an effect on test scores, and do better.

The passage I found was about a grizzly bear, and it was a really straightforward passage. So I thought, *It is just about grizzly bears and their habitat. This is the most simple natural science reading passage.* I had her read it out loud to me because I was checking for her decoding skills. If you can't decode, then you can't comprehend. She read the passage out loud to me, and she read it perfectly. Not a single mistake. I starting thinking, *Yes, this is finally going to happen.* Then she went to answer the questions, and I stayed excited. She was doing everything right, and she even stayed within the time limit and answered all the questions before time ran out. When I went to check them, I was so thrilled.

And she got all of the questions wrong—all of them.

I remember being so devastated. I didn't want to tell her her score after all the work we had put in, and it was on what I thought had been like the easiest passage that I could find. She gets them all wrong. I'm about to destroy this girl's confidence—my worst fear as a teacher. Once you do that, you create a learned helplessness that can spiral. I didn't end up telling her her exact score. I did communicate that it wasn't where we wanted to be, but I asked her a few questions. I wanted her feedback. *What did she not understand? What happened? How could I help her?*

Her response was, "Ms. Henly, what in the world is a grizzly bear?"

And that's when I realized that she had absolutely no cultural context for what she was reading about in that passage. When the test was asking about the author's purpose, or the author's choices to develop purpose, or organization, she had nothing in her background knowledge to give her any context to answer those questions or to understand this passage at all. One of the best reading intervention strategies is to visualize what you read, and if you can't do that, you don't understand it. We have people going into these standardized tests who have no cultural context what the passage is even about.

It wasn't her lack of knowledge for purpose or rhetorical analysis. No, absolutely not. It had nothing to do with her ability to execute the skills. It just happened to be that luck of the draw that she was reading about something that she couldn't visualize because she had no personal experience with that at all. Never even once. I think that's one of the big downfalls of standardized tests. No matter how hard we try, as long as we continue to test every child the exact same way, you cannot avoid situations like that.

One of the things that's excellent about college is that it's a collaborative learning environment. No matter where you go—public, private, community—it is collaborative. You have seminars, and you discuss, and you help each other figure things out. It is just like when we go out into the real world and have to figure problems out in our society. If she had run into this passage in college, and she was going to be tested over it, she would have had the opportunity to self advocate and ask for help. She would have had peers to run ideas by, and she would have been able to go to office hours to get extra help. And she was the student who was always doing that in my class. She was always staying after school with me trying to get better and figure stuff out, and it had paid off. She was ready for college.

I think that on a systemic level, we really need to stop testing every child the same way. When we are looking at the success and failure of our education system, we cannot see them as a lump of scores, but as different groups. One of them could be English language learners. You could look at their growth instead of a one-time score. Getting rid of standardized tests is not an option. We might need to consider that, but on a systemic level, we might consider looking at teacher input. This includes letters of recommendation to evaluate growth. This requires a community attitude shift toward teachers. That is one of the things that I feel constantly as a teacher.

The teacher evaluation system puts so much emphasis on test scores, and I feel very untrusted. I have to be checked all the time to make sure I'm doing my job when I would be doing a much better job if I didn't have to spend so much time doing that. Luckily in Kentucky, teachers aren't graded on test scores. But at the end of the day, if I were to be compared to other teachers that teach to a different population than I do in the same course, I might look like I'm not a very good teacher. This wouldn't be because of my skills but just because of the pure different situations that we are teaching in. If I'm being compared to a teacher who's teaching in an affluent community with people who are native English speakers, people that have always come from a place of privilege, and then you compare it to a teacher who teaches a very diverse population with all kinds of cultural, ethnic, and socioeconomic backgrounds, our scores are going to look very different. They are not a reflection of knowledge, they are a reflection of where you've come from. This is the unaccounted tragedy.

The Parent
Paul

"I see my kids being responsible adults that are really successful because as a parent, I want them to go beyond me."

I have five kids total, but I have two left in high school—a senior and a junior. They are trying to become college and career ready. They are also in band. They are involved in their church and their community. They are exceptional girls that I'm proud of.

I grew up here. There has definitely been more resources for my kids than when I was in high school. I graduated from here in '91. There's way more. There's so many ways they can go for their education. I didn't hear about GEAR UP when I was in high school. And there seems more of a push for them to get ready.

I went to Eastern Kentucky University for two years. I was undeclared, though I did have help because I was in the Upward Bound program. I was in the first year of that, and they kinda helped me through the process of what I needed to do to get to college. When I grew up, I never had anybody that ever went to college. I was the first to go to college. I have five other siblings, and none of them ended up going to college.

My daughters weren't really kids that I had to discipline much at all. They always pretty much listened. They had goals, and they wanted to impress their teachers. They didn't really want to get in trouble or anything like that. They would want to just stay in their books and study.

When they took the ACT test last Saturday, they told me that they felt they did well this time compared to the last time. They are at around a twenty-two or twenty-three. I don't know if they weren't feeling well last time they took it, or they just didn't do too well. They did say something, that they went to a room at school and they had some prep. They didn't really explain too much more about it. A lot of times, I'm not home, and they'll tell my wife. They're independent.

Basically, my kids know the cost of college. Well, we both do. If they kept their grades up, they would get their scholarships. They're trying to get their grades up for scholarships. Whatever we can help with, we'll help with. I feel like they're still in the process of completing the FAFSA. Is that what it's called? I don't know—it was just recently they started to fill it out. You know we give them the information they need to send to, but as with everything, it's stressful. You do what you gotta do.

Schools should give us more information to read through, any information that would help us make a smoother transition with our kids to college. I can't really find any other way. I haven't really talked to any other people to make it a smoother transition for the paperwork so they can get their financial needs taken care of. I mean, they have counselors at the school.

College is for them to get their education and try to find a job that they can do that they're going to appreciate. You're not just going for nothing. You're going for something, so you can advance that career that you're leaning towards and open up doors that would make it harder if you didn't go to college.

I see my kids being responsible adults that are really successful because as a parent, I want them to go beyond me. I really believe they're going to be responsible. They could be world changers. I really believe it.

The Parent
Dylan

"We need parents involved, and we need to get them comfortable in school buildings— not just parents, guardians too."

First of all, you have to be able to define college readiness for each student, and that can be very challenging, so then you try to generalize, and then when you generalize, you leave people behind. We need parents involved, and we need to get them comfortable in school buildings—not just parents, guardians too.

I work for the city. I'm a building inspector, and I make sure it's all under code. For example, no broken windows, and if a building is abandoned, I have it boarded up, and just different things. The students go in these abandoned buildings, and they party and they drink. So now I get to go shut these buildings down and force them to participate in other ways.

In our school, we had over two-hundred students identified as homeless, and we know what that means. Their parents were removed, and they had to go live with their uncle or aunt. So we have those kind of dynamics.

The transient students are what's changed here. When I went to school here, we were able to have pride. Like, for example someone older than us, a family member, went to the same school we did. Whereas nowadays, you'll have a kid that got kicked out of another school and comes here. Their parents didn't go here. They don't care about the community or the school the way we would have. So there's a lack of pride there, so you know that's very heavy in the school. Very heavy. I know a lot of the students, and just having that dynamic makes it tough.

So there are a lot of variables to that definition of college readiness. And I found that dealing with these students is that you'll have some students that are the typical college ready student. They do well in school—3.5 GPA, twenty-two on their ACT—they have the family background. You know, for some students though, it just means getting over the high school hump, maybe taking a break, getting a job, and then matching that up later with a college schedule where they can work and go to school. So we have to broaden the meaning of college readiness.

I have four in high school, two that graduated. I have one that graduated in 2011, my daughter. She was a Governor's Scholar by the way. My son was a 2013 grad. He's at Thomas More College playing football. I have two twin boys who are seniors.

I would describe my seniors as not prepared. I look at it 'em based on how I grew up. See, I had to look after myself, but see, they have parents. Me and my wife have been married for twenty-six years. Together since eighth grade. They look, and dad got a college degree, and mom's a nurse. So they come from a background where their parents are educated. They can slack where I couldn't, and it's frustrating as a parent. I think like, *Wow, y'all don't get it. Y'all don't know what it means to take care of yourself because you had parents.* And for my kids, that has been their handicap.

One thing I want to give is one thing we're fighting, which is "social construction." Take this word with you. No matter what you do as a parent, the kids your kids hang around, those people shape them whether they like it or not, or know it or not. So it's important we know that word, "social construction," because who they be around—their peers, their teachers that are involved in their life—in one way or another, in one shape or another, for positive or negative. It's not just about what's at home. If a lot of parents are not aware of social construction, they are at a handicap at protecting their kids.

One of my kids did well on the ACT; one didn't do so well. There is not necessarily a correlation between scores and college performance because with my kids, it'll come down to growin' up—maturity. It comes down to how well you can manage your time in college. I got a lot of time. What am I going to do with my time—that sort of thing. How they use the time. Oh, they're gonna go to college. Things work out.

I think college is for training. Training to deal with the outside world as you become an adult. Training as you become that age. Training—it gives you a wealth of knowledge. Biology, chemistry, English. All of that gives you a well-rounded perspective on how to deal with the world. But to be honest, it's not even education. Because to be honest, some of that information is outdated.

College ready, university ready, trade ready—all of those are a factor now 'cause some students aren't gonna go to a traditional college, you know. But to be ready means to be well-rounded and ready to survive in the society that you live in. Being able to know where you need to go to find the information you need to be successful. So being college ready just means being prepared for the college world and the outside world.

I see my kids being productive citizens the way me and my wife have taught them. Then, whatever they have picked up, you know how to drop off the negative, pick up the positive things. I would say there's a difference between being smart and intelligent. I would say my boys are going to be intelligent men. Because being smart just means you can recall information. You have the ability to see information and retain it. Intelligent means you can retain that information and use that information to make your life better. So I see them as being intelligent men when they get older.

The Village

The Parents, the Counselor & the Principal

"I wish my son could see the opportunity that he has in high school to learn all he can will help him in college, but he doesn't see that. He just wants to put in his seven hours and be done."

We facilitated this roundtable with parents and school staff in a small, rural school at the same time we held another one with students in a nearby classroom. We were grateful for the adults' seeming candor, but wondered throughout whether their stories would match up with the ones being shared next door.

• • •

Karen: My son is sixteen. He's a junior. He began the GEAR UP program, I believe it was in seventh grade. He has a younger brother who is in eighth grade. As far as I know, my youngest hasn't had any GEAR UP contact. Most recently, we moved here from out of state. We were looking for a place to set up a homestead and become farmers and live off the land. We happen to have family here, and it seemed like the land prices were just up our alley, so we came here. This was twenty-two years ago.

Victoria: My son is a junior this year, and he's sixteen.

Ben *(married to Victoria)*: I was born in Kentucky. I'm going to die in Kentucky. Between the two, I'm going to live. We moved to this county in '76, so I started high school here in this county. I was in sixth grade when we moved down here, so it's about time to be accepted as native. Students here now have a lot more variety. They have a lot more to do. The school has grown a lot—physically and in what they offer. Pretty much when I was here, they'd herd them in and herd them out. They'd talk three hours, and then they'd dismiss them. There seems to be a lot more opportunities now than when I was in school. Of course, I had to take advantage of opportunities that I had at the time, and we're having a bit of trouble trying to get our son to grasp the concept of the opportunities as presented to him. Pretty much, he just wants to get out and move on in life, but he's going to be ill prepared for it.

Victoria: I grew up in Green County, and then we got together and moved back here, what? Fourteen years ago?

Ben: Well, we spent some time in Louisville chasing jobs. Then when our son was born, we didn't want to be in Jefferson County Schools. It's metro, it's urban, huge classes, huge schools. Since he's an only child, we wanted him to have some kind of base, so he did his whole elementary school here, did his high school here so he will be able to look back on childhood friends. One of my best friends is somebody I went to school with, so he's basically a lifelong friend, somebody I can count on. So since he doesn't have siblings that have to help him move, he has to make some friends that will help him move.

Felicity: My son is a junior. We also have another son who is a freshman at Campbellsville University. I have a daughter who is a third grader, and I have twins who are four. I work with GEAR UP. I'm originally from the next county over, but my husband is from here, and we are the eighth generation of farmers on our farm. We're organic farmers.

Sharon: I only have one kid in this high school. I also have a daughter, she's in Northern Kentucky, and another son, he's in Richmond. My daughter started school, but she dropped out, and she's gone back. My older son, he tried a semester, but he didn't make it. My son here is a sophomore. Now he wants to go to school. He's not the same way. He loves school, it's all he talks about. He takes it seriously. He is very detail oriented. He has Asperger's Disorder, so he's very intelligent. He wants to make straight A's. He wants to do well. He's one of these kids, he's very driven. He wants to do well.

Felicity: My son is very intelligent. He lacks self-motivation, but he doesn't understand, "If it's not interesting to me at this very moment, why do I have to do it?" But his natural abilities far exceed what he shows. He has postsecondary plans. He's making plans to go to EKU. They have a wildlife management program, and a federal government job will be right up his alley. He's on academic team. You can ask him any date about any war. Any useless information! But he cannot brush his teeth every morning! A typical boy.

Ben: Ours is a typical sixteen-year-old boy. Motivation levels are not as high as I'd like to see 'em. He's probably going to graduate in the top eighty percent of his class. He'll be closer to the back than the front, but he is going to graduate. He's rather a smart kid. But he'll do anything he wants to and nothing he doesn't want to. He's got plans for postsecondary education, but it will all fall into place at the last minute. There's no planning ahead. There's no goal. It will happen when the time comes.

Victoria: He used to want to be an attorney until he realized how much schooling that would require, so now he's decided accounting is much better. He makes A's and B's, and he could make straight A's if he would try. But he very seldom opens a book.

Ben: Typical boy. I was the same way. Pretty much school's something you gotta do to get it over with and get done. There was not really a college aspiration when I graduated. But he just, he doesn't see the big picture because he's a kid!

Karen: Well my son is a typical sixteen-year-old. He's kind of an enigma, and he enjoys the fact that he's an enigma. He likes to keep us guessing. He's very motivated if it's something interesting to him. There definitely needs to be, not necessarily a fire lit under him, but there needs to be a spark somewhere for him to grasp hold of, and he doesn't really have big ambitions. But he has such natural ability to do anything he wants, and I think he's aware of that, which is good for his self-esteem. But also, at the same time, I think it holds him back, and he doesn't really want to reach for things too much. He wants to go to college one day, and the next day he doesn't, but I think that's just more to spite me. I'm pushing him in different directions. He's a philosopher right now, so he's just going all over the place with his ambition and just—he loves learning. He loves learning anything.

Kenna (*guidance counselor*): I was surprised. My son is a sophomore, and he had a twenty in science on the practice ACT. I'm like, where did that come from? I thought he would do better in math, but he didn't, so he has some work to do. The kids were supposed to receive a copy of their scores, of their sheet.

Victoria: Our son brings home nothing. I thought the teachers hadn't sent anything.

Kenna: With the practice, we just communicate through the students. But with the real ACT, we communicate with the parents. A lot of times, of course, on the sheet when they receive it, everything tells where they're weak, where they're lacking, and a lot of times, the kids will go up to their teachers, they actually will, for help. But sometimes, to interpret the scores, parents will come in. I saw a lot of surprises on the ACT. Students that you would think, when I go over their grades, and I sat down one on one with them and I say, "Look, you've got to stay on Wednesday and do my tutoring. You've got to do these things or we're going to have the same conversation at Christmas." And they get a twenty-four on their ACT. And I'm like, "What are you doing all day in class because you just made twenty-four on the ACT!" And then I've got students who just see it as a practice ACT and they just do a lot of bubbling. This particular ACT, I was surprised at how well my students, some of my personal advisees, did compared to their progress reports for the first few weeks of school. I think their ACT would be a better predictor of college success because I think the ACT is a nationally recognized test on a college level, but I can't tell you that in a school setting that if you make all A's in this school that you'll be successful wherever you go.

Sharon: My son doesn't test well. He has a disability, but he does get extended time. And I know there was something he took last year which I was really shocked about because when he looked at the ones he did answer, he did really well. But even with extended time, he over-thinks, and he does everything three times to make sure he gets the correct answer, and he runs out of time.

Kenna: I'm surprised he didn't come home and tell you about this one because he had his extended time, and he took quite a bit of time.

Sharon: He took his time, I know he did.

Karen: My son has taken the ACT three times, I think, and he's off the charts. It's a standardized test, I understand, and there are certain things like the math, which is a cumulative thing that he wouldn't be able to get such a high score on until he's a senior. His grades in school, they've just always been good. It comes easily to him and he enjoys it. So in terms of the standardized test, I think it is a skill to be able to take a standardized test, and if you can master that skill then that is definitely a plus in your book because a lot of the world is going to recognize you in standardized form. It's sad but true.

Felicity: Success is measured in a couple of different things. What I'm talking about is success in the classroom. Being successful in college is more than just being successful in the classroom. You can do really good on the ACT, but if I don't set my alarm on my phone and get to class then I won't retain the information I need to be successful, and that's where your soft skills come in.

Karen: I think college is an awesome opportunity that everyone should take advantage of if possible. My son agrees with me; I know he does. It's just a broadening of your perspective in general, and I don't think it could harm anybody, whether it's through your learning or interaction with other students or faculty. You're just enlarging your perspective on the world, and that's what college is all about to me, and I think my son agrees with me there. The career readiness part of it, I think that's why most people go to college, so they can get a good job and be successful with their lives because they have the financial backing to support their lifestyle and be happy and all that kind of stuff. I think he just has to want to and I think he does.

Victoria: To me, college means a better, more productive life. To my son it means, *How much money am I going to make?* I wish he could see the opportunity that he has in high school to learn all he can will help him in college, but he doesn't see that. He just wants to put in his seven hours and be done.

Ben: There are kids coming out of high school that are well rounded, good, and ready to take on life. There's going to be some that won't be able to cook an egg and everything in between. And this goes for lifestyle from the beginning. You may have some overprotective parents that guard their kid. You may have parents that are overly religious and they raise up a different kid. You may have parents that just don't care, the kid has to fend for themselves. A kid can come from the lousiest conditions and be a success, and a kid can come from the greatest conditions and be a failure. There's so many variables. Correlation is not causation.

But me personally, I didn't go to college. I went out into the workforce, got a job, got another job, got another job. Then I went back to school and got a technical degree which allowed me to get a better job and a better job and a better job. So I do have the technical degree. It's not much. It's pretty basic but it has opened doors that wouldn't have been open to me before, so college, postsecondary education, technical school is important, but not everyone is going to be an academic.

Not everyone is going to be a white collar worker; not everyone is going to wear a suit. You have to have people who work on cars, and you have to have people who work in factories. A blue collar life is not something to look down upon. It's not something to be shunned or sneered at. I've made a pretty decent life for my family by working in maintenance.

We've lost a lot of our manufacturing base, and we are more product and service-driven, so college is going to be important or some sort of postsecondary training. But when it comes down to it, things are going to break, and there's gonna be people that need to fix 'em. If nobody knows how to fix 'em, then our consumer culture is going to fail because there's no products there. You've gotta have people to put air conditioners in. You gotta have people to build homes.

Victoria: Or a plumber! How hard is it to find a plumber! I told my son, "You don't have to go to college, that's fine! But you're going to have some kind of postsecondary education where you can provide for yourself and your family. I don't care if that means you are a plumber because you make a house call and twenty-five bucks to just go and make a house call!" It's probably more than that now.

Ben: It's more than that now.

Victoria: You know, I told him, "That's your choice. You're going to do something, and you will have to have some education once you get out."

Ben: There's a man I know, he's the same age as I am. We would have graduated the same year. I never met him as a child because he dropped out in seventh grade. Dropped out, went to work on the farm. A local farm boy. I went to school, graduated, job, married, another job, went back to school, technical degree, better job, better job, better job. This seventh grade dropout from the sweat of his brow, being an astute business man, owns about six farms, hundreds of heads of cattle, grows lots of tobacco, lots of hay, lots of corn. Tractors, trucks, and I don't know if he ever went back and got his GED or not, but the point is, a seventh grade dropout, everything is stacked against you, but the man made himself a success. Provided a good living for his family, just by the sweat of his brow and common sense, whereas there are college graduates who don't have common sense. There are people who can't survive outside of academia!

It's like my momma, she dropped out of school in sixth grade. Of course, it was a different time. And she went to work in a restaurant. She went back and she would have got her GED back in the early '80s I think. Education was important to mom and dad. They said, "All our kids are going to finish high school." Postsecondary? Well, dad was a truck driver. He's been a mechanic. He'd done a lot of other things. He was a blue-collar worker, so I think going to college wasn't as prevalent. People who are white-collar, their kids, they expect them to go to college because it was part of their lives and their upbringing and how they made a success of themselves. Whereas, for a blue-collar worker, it's a little different. You want to go to college, great, maybe you can learn something that will help you out. But I don't think it's as pressing in rural areas as maybe it would be in a high-end urban setting. If our boy says he wants to go to school, it will happen. I said, "How are you going to pay for college?" He said, "Aren't you going to pay for it?" I said, "The United States Military."

The Principal: My experience as a student and my experience as an educator is I have seen students go to college and fall flat on their faces because they didn't have to apply themselves in high school. They knew how to work the system. They had the grades, but they did not have the foundation, and you've got to have the foundation, or the building is gonna crumble. We call this term "persistence." It's one thing to get kids into postsecondary education out of high school, but what are we doing to keep them there? A lot of them, we're losing. In all honesty, what we see in this school and others, 'cause the students come to us all the time, we see that all they need is to hear it from somebody else. And when they hear it from somebody else, it kinda seals the cracks in that foundation. It teaches them how to seal the cracks in the foundation because they're scared. They don't know how to manage it. They look at it as obstacles. And then with a little bit of guidance and reinforcement, they create the solution. There was the problem, and they create the solution.

Afterword

Like anyone else attempting to understand the issue, I scrutinized the Kentucky Department of Education's college readiness reports for individual schools, and thought they provided a pretty clear picture. But it wasn't until I stumbled upon the data for my own school that the image suddenly became blurry:

- Thirty-seven percent of the students are not college or career ready,
- Thirty-two percent of Hispanic students are college going,
- Forty-two percent of students on free and reduced lunch are college going.*

As a high school senior, I felt I knew my school intimately, but reading these particular numbers left so many questions unanswered.

Were the same students I passed each day in the hallway among that thirty-seven percent who are not considered college or career ready? Did the thirty-two percent of Hispanics in my school who are expected to go to college include Marina or Nicholas? And if Bella was part of that forty-two percent on free and reduced lunch, why should that determine her whole future?

I felt as though the cold data sold my classmates and me short, reducing us to faceless figures instead of living human beings. Still, I—and many of the students who worked on this book—are proud math and science geeks. We weren't ready to reject the numbers altogether.

So in addition to the interviews and roundtables we collected and shared in the previous pages, we decided to design our own quantitative study. We crafted a 130-question survey and disseminated it to 450 seniors in five high schools representing the geographic diversity of the state and included the questions that we, as people ourselves on the cusp of high school graduation, wanted to know.

By directing our attention to a few priority issues, the numbers underscore elements of the narratives that we think are especially urgent for those with decision-making power to note.[†] More specifically, when it comes to college readiness, we found:

1. **Too many students in Kentucky are not sold on the value of college.** A full forty percent of Kentucky seniors we surveyed indicated they believe that college is not necessary to be successful. The main reason students responding to our survey said they had decided not to go to college was because they felt they wanted to or needed to have a full time job.

2. **Family support has a significant impact on students pursuing a degree, yet too many Kentucky students feel they don't have it.** Of the students we surveyed, twenty percent reported that they do not feel like they have either a parent or guardian that cares about their academic performance.

3. **The primary tool to measure college readiness reflects and possibly even perpetuates inequity.** Of the students we surveyed who took test prep classes outside of school, eighty-four percent reported having higher ACT scores. Those who didn't take the classes though cited expenses and lack of time or needing to work as primary obstacles while fifteen percent of students reported to us that they didn't take the ACT more than once only because they couldn't afford it. And it's probably worth noting too that seventeen percent of the students we surveyed reported suffering from testing anxiety from a majority of the time to every single time.

4. **Kentucky has a school counseling crisis.** Half of the Kentucky high school seniors we surveyed reported feeling like they have not had a meaningful discussion about steps to college or career readiness with a counselor. And worse, twenty-five percent of the students we surveyed report never having discussed college or future plans with any adult in their school building at all.

Afterword

If I had to sum up our findings, I'd say that what we discovered in the combination of our survey analysis and conversations, the heart and the head of our work, is that college readiness—and school in general—is about so much more than academics alone.

I still cannot get over how nearly every student we met, in every situation, seemed surprised and grateful to have us ask for feedback on their education. The responsibility I in turn felt to share their stories was punctuated by students like Emma who approached me after our interview and earnestly asked, "Are you going to do something about this, or are you like the people in suits that pretend they care and then disappear from our lives?"

Six months after my interview with Brianna, I found myself exchanging texts about her day. When I brought up the progress our team has made with the book, she texted back:

> "It's so good… it's so real it's scary, but if someone doesn't say it who will?"

Such reactions speak to the absurdity of how in school, we talk about everything but school itself.

I hope if nothing else, the stories students shared with us in *Ready or Not* spark the intergenerational conversations that forever challenge that. Students have so much to offer in the efforts to make our schools better, if only we will listen.

Sahar Mohammadzadeh
Executive Editor

Acknowledgments

This book is the direct result of a statewide collaborative effort for which we have many people to thank.

We are first and foremost grateful to Prichard Committee staff: Executive Director, Brigitte Blom Ramsey; Associate Director, Cory Curl; Senior Policy Director, Perry Papka; Strategic Communications Director, Michael Andrews; Operations, Events, and Marketing Director, Michelle Whitaker; Development Director, Suzetta Yates; Grants and Finance Coordinator, Melody Brooks; Program Associate, Alana Morton, and out-of-retirement-just-for-us Office Manager, Pam Shepherd, for reviewing our work at every turn and for providing critical moral and technical support throughout the research and writing process. We also appreciate their tolerance for numerous office conference room takeovers, replete with whiteboard wipe outs and oversized pizza boxes.

We treasure our collaboration with the Council for Postsecondary Education and GEAR UP Kentucky, led by CPE's President Robert King and Dr. Aaron Thompson and GUK's Bruce Brooks, Dawn Offut, Wendy Nealy, Victoria Andrew and Omari Gletten for believing so deeply in the power of student voice from the beginning. We reserve extra gratitude for Kim Drummond, who rolled up her sleeves and spent untold energy plotting, planning, and coordinating everything in uncanny sync with our crazy hours and ideas.

Special thanks to administrators and teachers, GEAR UP College and Career Readiness Counselors, and GEAR UP Students of the Year for coordinating so many of our site visits. Specifically, thanks to: Newport Independent High School's Stacey Schneller, Denise Jason, Kyle Niederman, and Samara Hall; Hart County High School's James Fitzstephens, Forrest Wise, Ferol Hawkins, Lisa Willian, Greg Cecil, and Rachel

McIntire; Owen County High School's Marie Cobb, Denise Finley, Duane Kline and Jessica Hardin; Trigg County High School's Sheila Thomas, Kerry Sweno, Denise Craft, Audrey Neal, Cammie Evans, Shannon Burcham, and Summer Cottrell; and Fleming County High School's Cindy Jolly, Sarah Jones, Beth Lawson, Stephanie Emmons, and Emily Steele, for the courage to open your doors to us with our unfiltered questions. We acknowledge the challenges inherent in teaching against a sometimes college-resistant culture. And though some educators succumb to it, as these stories have shown, we appreciate the valiant efforts of these people and so many others in their schools who instead inspire students to see that education is freedom.

We deeply appreciate our University of Kentucky School of Education champions, Drs. Lu Young, Justin Bathon, Carmen Coleman, Linda France, and John Nash for laying the academic groundwork to support meaningful student voice as a critical component of effective schools and for serving as a collective and critical academic sounding board without dampening either our enthusiasm—or our ambition.

Thanks too to our research mentors, Drs. Patty Kannapel and Michael Flory of CNA Analysis and Solutions, for providing gentle guidance on the original protocol and for helping us normalize, just enough, our otherwise radical research.

We would be lost—and without reliable parking or wifi—without Tonya Crum, Brian Spellman, Nancy Carpenter, Renee Shaw, Kenny Hamilton, and others from Kentucky Educational Television and are so appreciative of the space, technical assistance, and oversight provided for our many large gatherings. Our special relationship honors the spirit of the late Lynda Thomas, who did so much to establish it in the first place.

We are indebted to our own little village of sustained support—the teachers, administrators, counselors, youth development leaders, and parents who have championed our work throughout and beyond this project: Stan Torzewski, Kip Hottman, Holly Wood, Thad Elmore, MeMe Ratliff, Brad Clark, Will Nash, Bjorn Wastvedt, Brison Harvey, Deanna Smith, Kiara James, Judith Bradley, Jane Shropshire, Dr. Heidi T. Abell, Tabitha Dillinger, Ben Reno-Weber, Beth Malcom, Angie Allen, Shana Burg, Molly Toney, and Cindy Baumert. At various times, they helped us reach some of the harder-to-reach students, encouraged us through challenging moments, and showed what is possible when youth and adults work together as full partners.

This book is inspired by the work of the late Robert Clampitt with Lynn Sygiel and the teen editors of Children's Express who provided a model with *When I Was Young I Loved School*, their groundbreaking youth-led investigation into the school dropout crisis a generation ago.

Ready or Not would not be ready at all without the generous contributions of the State Farm Youth Advisory Board and the Lumina Foundation and its Strategy Labs. Among other things, their financial investment in us gave us crucial, early credibility.

Finally, and most importantly, we extend our profound gratitude to the hundreds of students we talked with from across Kentucky for so courageously and honestly sharing their lives with us. Though we will try to repay them in some form as we disseminate their stories and make sure they are heard, we already know that we cannot ever thank them enough.

Glossary

ACT: College readiness assessment; includes English, mathematics, reading and science; taken by all Kentucky eleventh grade students; included in high schools' scores for Next Generation Learners.

ACT WorkKeys: Workplace skills assessment; includes applied mathematics, locating information, and reading for information; not required for Kentucky students.

Advanced Placement (AP): Exams that can earn students college credit or placement in upper-level college courses based on proven learning during high school; AP courses are classes designed to qualify students to take AP exams; similar to the IB and Cambridge Advanced International programs; offered in many Kentucky schools.

Armed Services Vocational Aptitude Battery (ASVAB): Assessment to determine military eligibility; includes arithmetic reasoning, word knowledge, paragraph comprehension, and mathematics knowledge; not required, but successful student results can be used for the readiness comonent of a high school's score for Next Generation Learners.

Cambridge Advanced International: An international curriculum and evaluation system preparing students for college; similar to the AP and IB programs; offered in some Kentucky schools.

Career Ready: Defined by the Kentucky Board of Education to be high school graduates which have met benchmarks for academics, with the Armed Services Vocational Aptituted Battery (ASVAB) or ACT WorkKeys, or technical, with the Kentucky Occupational Skills Standards Assessments (KOSSA) or industry-recognized certification. Kentucky's definition of Career Ready will change after the 2017-18 school year.

College and Career Ready (CCR): Students which have achieved both College and Career Readiness as defined by the Council on Postsecondary Education; used to refer to postsecondary readiness in general; also known as Future Ready.

College Ready: Defined by the Council on Postsecondary Education to be high school graduates which have met benchmarks for the ACT, SAT, KYOTE, or another exam. For the 2017-18 school year, the ACT benchmarks are eighteen on English, nineteen on mathematics, and twenty on reading; students not meeting benchmark take remedial courses in the subject at state universities. Kentucky's definition of College Ready will change after the 2017-18 school year.

Council on Postsecondary Education (CPE): State-level council that provides direction for Kentucky's public universities, community colleges and technical schools, and adult education; council members are nominated by the governor and confirmed by the legislature; the Council's members hire and evaluate their president.

Dual credit course: A college-level course in which a high school student can earn both high school and college credit.

End-of-Course Exam (EOC): Assessment measuring student learning in a particular course; English II, Algebra II, Biology and US History. End-of-Course Exams are part of K-PREP and required for high school students; results of those four assessments can be part of students' final grades in the course and are used as part of their school's score for Next Generation Learners.

Free Application for Federal Student Aid (FAFSA): A form that can be prepared annually by current and prospective college students, both undergraduate and graduate, in the United States to determine their eligibility for student financial aid.

GEAR UP: A coordinated effort between middle schools, high schools, colleges and universities to support and encourage low-income middle and high school students to pursue postsecondary education; supported by federal grants; short for Gaining Early Awareness and Readiness for Undergraduate Education Programs.

General Educational Development Diploma (GED): Diploma or equivalency certificate awarded to adults after passing an exam certifying they have mastered certain skills and knowledge in reading, writing, social studies, science, and mathematics; adult education programs offer GED classes to prepare students for taking the exam; equivalent to a high school diploma.

Grade Point Average (GPA): A number, usually on a 4.0 scale, representing an average of a student's grades either for the semester, year, or multiple school years.

Individual Learning Plan (ILP): A plan for each student mapping out steps to graduation and success based on academic and career interests. Starting in sixth grade, all Kentucky public school students create and update ILPs with input from their parents and educators. The ILP replaces earlier requirements for an individual graduation plan.

International Baccalaureate (IB): Rigorous international program of studies and examinations, recognized by one hundred countries for university admission; includes study of languages, humanities, mathematics, and science; similar to the AP or Cambridge Advanced International programs; offered in some Kentucky schools

Kentucky Board of Education: Eleven-member state board responsible for preschool to high school education; sets policy, adopts regulations, grants waivers, and hires and evaluates the commissioner of education; members appointed by the governor and confirmed by the legislature.

Kentucky Educational Excellence Scholarship (KEES): A program providing college scholarships based on students' ACT scores and grade point averages; students eligible for free or reduced-price lunch during any year of high school can earn supplmental awards for Advanced Placement, International Baccalurete, and Cambridge Advanced International scores; funded with Kentucky lottery revenue.

Kentucky Education Reform Act (KERA): 1990 legislation reorganizing all elements of Kentucky education from preschool through grade twelve.

Glossary

Kentucky Occupational Skill Standards Assessments (KOSSA): Online assessment of workplace skills using multiple choice and a problem-based open-ended question; not required, but successful student sresults can be used for the readiness component of a high school's score for Next Generation Learners.

Kentucky Online Testing (KYOTE): An online assessment used by most Kentucky colleges and universities to determine course placement for entering students not meeting ACT benchmarks; not required, but successful student results can be used for the readiness component of a high school's score for Next Generation Learners.

Kentucky Performance Rating for Educational Progress (K-PREP): Required state assessments of reading, mathematics, science, social studies, writing and language mechanics; uses constructed response items and multiple choice questions, plus an on-demand writing prompt; includes the multiple-choice portion of the required End-of-Course Exams; a major factor in schools' scores for Next Generation Learners

Limited English proficiency (LEP): Dscriptive term for students who speak another language and know little or no English. Students are enrolled in an English as a Second Language (ESL) or English Language Learner (ELL) class.

Next Generation Learners: For school accountability in Kentucky, the portion of a school or district's Overall Score that reflects student performance by combining components for achievement, gap group, growth, readiness and graduation.

Preliminary SAT/National Merit Scholarship Qualifying Test (PSAT/NMSQT): A standardized test administered by the College Board and cosponsored by the National Merit Scholarship Corporation in the United States; modled off of and prepares students for the SAT; not required in Kentucky.

SAT: College readiness assessment; includes reading, mathematics, and writing; taken by some students as an alternative or in addition to the ACT; not required in Kentucky; not included in high schools' scores for Next Generation Learners.

Find more education terms and concepts at prichardcommittee.org/edguides.

Notes

Preface

* "Kentucky Graduates Make Incremental Gains on the ACT," Kentucky Department of Education, August 24, 2016, archived at https://perma.cc/8X3W-SHV5.

† Karren M. Timmel et al., "A Look Inside Kentucky's College and Career Readiness Data" (Frankfort, KY: Office of Education Accountability, Legislative Research Commission), accessed August 4, 2017, archived at https://perma.cc/XA7A-K2YY.

‡ "College Persistence in Kentucky," Harvard Strategic Data Project, n.d., archived at https://perma.cc/RM7J-TEEW.

The Moonlighters

* Gucci is a slang term often meaning good or well, as in the high quality of the brand Gucci.

The Newcomers

* "2016-17 EL Language Chart," Spreadsheet (Kentucky Department of Education), accessed August 4, 2017, archived at https://perma.cc/X23W-5T62.

† "Kentucky Education Facts," Kentucky Department of Education, May 2, 2017, archived at https://perma.cc/W8QJ-VKUF.

‡ Christa Rounsavall, "Louisville Leads the Way in Refugee Resettlement," Louisville Distilled, April 26, 2016, archived at https://perma.cc/7ZVE-XVU2.

The Oddsbuckers

* Paul Skomsvold, "Profile of Undergraduate Students: 2011-12 (Web Tables)," Tables (National Center for Education Statistics, October 2, 2014), archived at https://perma.cc/NP5C-93DL.

† Kavitha Cardoza, "First-Generation College Students Are Not Succeeding in College, and Money Isn't the Problem," *The Washington Post,* January 20, 2016, archived at https://perma.cc/3HBY-KPRG.

Afterword

* Kentucky Center for Education and Workforce Statistics, "High School Graduating Class of 2015, Paul Laurence Dunbar High School, Fayette County" Kentucky High School Feedback Report on College Going (Frankfort, KY, n.d.), accessed August 30, 2017, archived at https://perma.cc/NKG9-HXAQ.

† The data from our original survey will be published on prichardcommittee.org.

Also by the Student Voice Team

Uncovering the Tripwires to Postsecondary Success

Student Voice Audit: Robert D. Clark Junior High School

*Students As Partners: Integrating Student Voice
in the Governing Bodies of Kentucky Schools*

Ready or Not: The Statistics Behind the Stories

Find these reports at:

prichardcommittee.org/resources

Made in the USA
Lexington, KY
07 June 2018